A SHORT GUIDE TO WRITING ABOUT HISTORY

...

Sixth Edition

RICHARD MARIUS
Late, Harvard University

MELVIN E. PAGE
East Tennessee State University

PEARSON
Longman

New York   San Francisco   Boston
London   Toronto   Sydney   Tokyo   Singapore   Madrid
Mexico City   Munich   Paris   Cape Town   Hong Kong   Montreal

Publisher: Joseph Opiela
Marketing Manager: Thomas De Marco
Production Manager: Denise Phillip
Project Coordination, Text Design, and Electronic Page Makeup: GGS Book
    Services, Inc.
Cover Designer/Manager: John Callahan
Cover Image: Copyright © Kazuyoshi Nomachi/Corbis
Senior Manufacturing Buyer: Alfred C. Dorsey
Printer and Binder: R. R. Donnelley & Sons—Harrisonburg
Cover Printer: Coral Graphic Services

For permission to use copyrighted material, grateful acknowledgment is made to
the copyright holders on page 233, which is hereby made part of this copyright
page.

Library of Congress Cataloging-in-Publication Data
Marius, Richard.
    A short guide to writing about history / Richard Marius, Melvin E. Page.—6th ed.
        p. cm.
    Includes bibliographical references and index.
    ISBN 0-321-43536-2
        1. Historiography.   2. History—Methodology.   3. History—Research.
    4. Academic writing.   I. Page, Melvin E. (Melvin Eugene), 1944–   II. Title.

D13.M294 2006
907.2—dc22   2006019009

Visit us at www.ablongman.com.

ISBN 0-321-43536-2

    4 5 6 7 8 9 10—DOH—09 08

For our children—
Richard, Fred, and John
Megan, Melanie, and Michael
And our adventures together exploring history,
at home and around the world.

CONTENTS

■ ■ ■

PREFACE TO THE SIXTH EDITION

■ ■ ■

Since its first edition, many college students have used *A Short Guide to Writing About History* in their adventures with writing history papers. I have always found it useful for my students as they have tried coming to grips with methods historians employ in research and writing about the past. More than that, the commitment of Professor Marius to such endeavors was unstinting. As he promised, those who wrote to him with questions were not disappointed; and on several different occasions he joined my entire class for organized listserv discussions of historical research and writing. His insights were always helpful and to the point for my students. And they certainly were important to me as I attempted to teach the excitement of historical study.

There is no question of the importance that Richard Marius had in shaping a new generation of historians. Following his untimely death in late 1999, editors at Longman were determined to keep his advice available for still more students in the twenty-first century. I was honored and pleased to prepare subsequent editions of this *Short Guide* and grateful for the conversations I previously had with Richard about this book, which helped me immeasurably in updating the work. In creating the sixth edition, I have myself been going back to Richard's advice even as I have tried to adapt it for a new generation of students. In addition to our passion about the study and writing of history, we both shared a great faith in the intelligence and tenacity—as well as the curiosity—of our student readers. I hope this edition continues to reflect that belief.

The sixth edition recognizes more than before how accelerating technological developments have not so much reshaped but rather reoriented research and writing efforts of almost all historians. Chapter 6, "Writing in an Electronic Age," especially, reflects more than any previous editions the impact of computers and the Internet on historians' work. At the same time, I have continued to ground advice to students on the same basic principles that both Professor Marius and I believe are the foundation of good historical writing. Dealing with this new environment, however, does require all historians to adapt their conventions, and this edition continues to reflect such change.

The emphasis of student capacities to improve their own writing is also reflected in updated "Writer's Checklists," including a new "Writer's Checklist for Peer Editing," which I hope will serve to encourage collaborative revision processes. In addition, continuing public discussions about the fundamental integrity of historical scholarship has led me to include an expanded discussion of the principle of original work and the problems of plagiarism, with suggestions about how to avoid that unpardonable sin of historical writing. And in response to requests for more examples of note and bibliographic citations, I have added two new reference charts that are keyed to the text of Chapter 8, which explains the basic principles for documenting sources.

As before, I am eager to hear from readers about experiences with this book. Please write to me with any thoughts you have about *A Short Guide to Writing About History*. Letters may be mailed to me at the History Department, East Tennessee State University, Johnson City, TN 34614. You may also send e-mails to, pagem@etsu.edu. As did Professor Marius, I shall always respond.

ACKNOWLEDGMENTS

A number of historians at various colleges and universities offered priceless advice in the preparation of the manuscript for various editions of *A Short Guide to Writing About History*. I am particularly grateful to those whose thoughtful comments helped shape this sixth edition: Alan Baumler, Indiana University of Pennsylvania; Sandra M. Frink, Roosevelt University; Cynthia Kosso, Northern Arizona University; Kriste Lindenmeyer, University of Maryland— Baltimore County; David John Marley, Vanguard University; Brian A. Pavlac, King's College; Jeff Roberts, Tennessee Technological University; Lee Shai Weissbach, University of Louisville; Kenneth Wilburn, East Carolina University; and Allan M. Winkler, Miami University.

I also appreciate the support I have had from colleagues at three universities where I have taught about historical writing and research: Murray State University, the University of Natal, Durban (South Africa), and East Tennessee State University. While all my colleagues have influenced my thinking about these subjects in one way or another, I especially appreciate conversations with Doug Burgess, Henry Antkiewicz, Daniel Newcomer, Steve Fritz, Charles Allan, and Myra Jones on many details concerning historical research and writing; our continued engagement with these issues has been especially important for the sixth edition. I have learned much, as well, from my students who shared with me their frustrations and triumphs in historical research and writing; Joe Gayeski, Justin Horton, Tabetha Garman, Bill Hembrock, and Sabrina Shilad have made specific contributions to this book. And I want especially to thank my former student, Penny Sonnenburg-Willis for crucial help in reshaping the advice concerning research and note-taking. At Longman Publishers, I appreciate the continued encouragement and confidence of Joseph Opiela and Whitney Baer.

Most of all, this edition would not be possible without the road laid down by Richard Marius years ago. Collaborators such as he are hard to find. I count myself fortunate indeed.

MELVIN E. PAGE

PREFACE TO
THE THIRD EDITION

■ ■ ■

This little book arose out of my experience of teaching European history for sixteen years—first at Gettysburg College and then at my alma mater, the University of Tennessee, Knoxville—and then out of the sixteen years I spent directing the Expository Writing Program at Harvard, where I regularly taught a course called "Writing About History."

Most students came into my courses believing that history was hardly more than a collection of names and dates to be memorized and repeated on examinations. They thought they could go to the library, look up several articles in encyclopedias, and write a paper to show how much they knew about a subject. They did not imagine that they could think for themselves about the facts. Sometimes they believed that "thinking" was to express vehement opinions, often about the supposed morality or immorality of the past they read and wrote about. Far too often they tried to write as though they were accomplished historians who had solved all the problems about some broad historical subject and could only scorn those who disagreed with them.

It was my job to teach them that history becomes most exciting when we study a collection of primary sources—the basic stuff from which history is made—to make sense of these sources and tell a story about them. Primary sources are by definition the sources closest to the events and people whose stories we seek to tell. They may be letters, diaries, and books published by participants in events. Woodrow Wilson, Thomas More, Martin Luther King Jr.,

Virginia Woolf, Eleanor Roosevelt, and Toni Morrison all wrote extensively or spoke so that their words were recorded by others. These written materials are primary sources for their lives. Or primary sources may be the earliest reports of those who knew or claimed to know figures in the past whom we study in the present.

Historians and others have written about these primary sources. They have produced secondary sources—narratives, interpretations, and descriptions—to tell us what they think the primary sources mean. These secondary sources, as we call them, embody hard work and careful thought—and often disagree with one another. No one serious about the study of history can neglect this treasury of research and thought, and students should demonstrate in the papers they write in college that they are familiar with what other people have written about a topic. The best history papers show a balance between primary and secondary sources.

The best reasons for studying history are the same as those for studying all the liberal arts: historical study satisfies curiosity, and it enriches our minds. The most interesting human beings are those with curiosity. They ask questions. How did things get to be the way they are? Why have some names come down to us glittering with fame or stained with infamy? Why is this monument here? Why was this painting a scandal when it was first shown to the public? How did this book cause a revolution? Who built this amazing bridge?

History also provides us with the pleasure of vicarious experience—living in our imaginations lives others have lived in the past. It opens windows into the variety of human experience and reveals human nature, not in some abstract philosophical way but in the concrete actuality of what real human beings thought and did. History tells us how diverse human beings and their societies can be. If we study it attentively, it should make us more tolerant of people unlike ourselves because history reveals such an immense variety of successful human experiences.

Teaching people to write about history has been for me a means of showing students of all ages that they have worthwhile thoughts and can use them to write interesting and original essays on many subjects. As users of this book will, I hope, discover, the study of history involves a special kind of thinking, closely related to the way we solve puzzles and try to guess who the murderer is in a good mystery. Historical thinking is indeed a kind of game, and it has a deeply serious side—but it is also a lot of fun!

I live and move and have my being in a circle of friends without whom nothing would be worthwhile. As I have done so many times in the past, I offer heartfelt thanks to a life that has brought me many friends, including my brother John, and my wife of almost thirty years, Lanier Smythe.

I hope *A Short Guide to Writing About History* will continue to help students think about history, see its puzzles and its pleasures, and gain the confidence that good writing about anything requires. You must approach the task with the trust that you have the tools to do the job, and I hope you will find them in this little book.

RICHARD MARIUS

WRITING AND HISTORY

. . .

Students struggling over an essay in history—for a book review, a full research paper, an examination, or even a short class assignment—have often told us that they know the subject, but they cannot write about it. In our experience this often means they have a jumble of facts and information in their heads but cannot tell a story about them.

Their complaint represents a discovery: History *does* involve telling a story, and while facts are essential in telling a story, they are not enough. If you know what armies faced each other, at what place, and who emerged victorious, you may not necessarily be able to tell a story about the encounter. Even if you know the names of the opposing commanders, and the various units under their command, it still may not be enough. Stories have tension, and while battles certainly have enough of that, you will need to sketch out the specific elements of that tension before readers will be engaged by your story. Why were the armies engaged against each other? What were their expectations should they emerge victorious? Readers will see the tensions, embrace the accounts of the struggle, and read on to see how it all comes out, not just who won and lost, but the implications of that outcome.

STORIES ABOUT THE PAST INTENDED TO BE TRUE

In writing about history, you tell the story of your thinking about a topic and formulate a central argument—or *thesis*—to say that things happened in a particular way and not another. You allow for the

1

possibility that if this or this, or that, did not happen, things could have turned out entirely differently. And you explain what resulted from the events unfolding as they did.

Historians are like most people: they want to know what events mean, why they were important to what came afterwards, and why we still talk about them. Like journalists, they ask *who, what, where, when,* and *why.* Who was responsible? What happened? Where did it happen? When and in what order did things happen? Why did they happen? And historians often ask additional questions, such as: What have other historians said about the event? What mistakes did they make that we can now correct? Historians are curious and relentless questioners, and the questions they ponder arise from any number of sources. All historical writing begins as an effort to answer questions about origins, happenings, and consequences. Historians find a puzzle and try to solve it. When you write for a history course, you must do the same—find a problem that stirs your curiosity and try to solve it. If you don't have a problem, you don't have a historical essay!

Here are the first two paragraphs of an article that appeared in *The American Historical Review,* the leading journal for historians in the United States:

> In 1908, an Iranian humanist sounded the bell of doom. Anticipating Iran's "last sigh," this writer—presumably Mu'ayyid al-Islam, the editor of the popular newspaper *Habl al-Matin*—railed against Russia's encroachment on Iran as well as its blatant disregard for human life. For this Iranian, the humanistic entreaties of the so-called "civilized, philanthropic govern-ments" of the West seemed little more than empty words—a point con-firmed by Russia's militaristic (and inhumane) drive south of its border. As he remarked, "In this new, bright age of humanism . . . in this age in which protection of fellow human beings is considered a requisite of humanity . . . our northern neighbor [Russia] has sent a military expedition to our soil without any right or grounds." Territorial threats from Russia, however, were nothing new for Iran. Why then, had Russia's recent advance so alarmed this writer?
>
> The answer lay in the Qajar dynasty's embrace of humanism and patriotic thinking. In this "bright, new age," in which Iran had celebrated

nationhood and the rule of law, it expected international recognition of its national sovereignty. Nothing proved more distasteful to this patriot than Russia's sheer disrespect for Iranians and their sacred homeland. The offensive meant that Iran, a country increasingly depicted as "sick" and on the verge of territorial and political demise, had yet to be accepted as a sovereign, "civilized" nation in the commonwealth of humanity. In short, Russia's invasion had flouted Iran's modernist ethos of humanism."[1]

The author, Professor Firoozeh Kashani-Sabet, was puzzled by the reactions to early twentieth-century Russian imperial ventures in Iran articulated in an Iranian newspaper. After American interventions in the Persian Gulf region in recent decades, the question of Russian incursions a century ago may seem far removed from our concerns about the region. Yet that puzzle interested Professor Kashani-Sabet, and she wrote an essay to solve it.

Solving the puzzles of history involves both science and art. Science is a synonym for knowledge. But knowledge of what? History includes data—evidence, the names of people and places, when things happened, where they happened, bits of information gathered from many sources. It also includes interpretations of historians and others in the past who have written on the topic that the writer decides to treat in an essay. The art of history lies in combining fact and interpretation to tell a story about the past, as Professor Kashani-Sabet did in her article.

Historians believe it is important to distinguish between the true and the false. Thus their stories, as the late Professor J. H. Hexter was fond of saying, are a "patterned, coherent account of the human past intended to be true,"[2] as distinguished from the fiction of novels and short stories, for example. In the sixteenth century some English writers called history "authentic stories" to distinguish it from fantastic tales about the past. Historians in the Renaissance searched for old

---

[1] Firoozeh Kashani-Sabet, "Hallmarks of Humanism: Hygiene and Love of Homeland in Qajar Iran," *The American Historical Review* 105 (2000): 1171. We have omitted Professor Kashani-Sabet's footnotes.

[2] J. H. Hexter, *The History Primer* (New York: Basic Books, 1971), 5.

documents, studied them to see if they were authentic, weeded out forgeries, and compared copies to find errors scribes had made in transmitting texts. They also compared different stories told about the same events. These historians tried to tell the truth—as do historians today.

But in the study of history, "truth" is complicated, contradictory, and often obscure. Every historical event happens one time and becomes separated from the present by the steady accumulation of other events happening day by day. We cannot put any incident from the past into a laboratory and make it happen again and again as we might conduct an experiment in chemistry, measuring and calculating to see precisely the relations of cause and effect. Instead, we must rely on evidence from the past such as memories of those who were there and objects from that time to guide us as we tell the story. But all these are mere records, subject to many interpretations and subject also to the tricks memory plays even on eyewitnesses. We can never relive the event exactly as it happened.

The evidence for past events is therefore always incomplete and fragmentary. Many pieces of evidence are lost, and others are often faded and warped. Historians fit the pieces together as carefully as possible, but holes remain in the picture they try to reconstruct. They do their best to fill in the holes with inferences that seem plausible and that fit the available facts. What emerges may closely resemble what happened, but we can never be completely sure that what we know as history is an exact replica of the past. Our knowledge of history is always in flux, and historians are always in dialogue, not only with the primary sources of the events they write about but also with other historians of those events.

WRITING HISTORY AS A WAY OF THINKING

History and writing are inseparable. We cannot know history well unless we write about it. Writing allows us to arrange events and our thoughts, study our work, weed out contradictions, get names and places right, and question interpretations, our own and those of other historians. In writing we work out the chronological order of events—not a simple task but one indispensable to the historian's craft. Fluent talkers, on the other hand, can touch on first one idea and then another, sometimes using body language to stress a point. They can overwhelm opposition by charisma or by shouting when their argument is weak. Writers perform a more daring act! They must develop an idea with logic and clarity, knowing that a reader can study their words again and again and discover whether the words add up to a plausible argument, given the evidence available. If writers are illogical, unfair, untruthful, confused, or foolish, their words lie on the page to be attacked by anyone with the care and interest to look. Good talkers can contradict themselves, waffle, and weasel, and on being called to task, can claim that their hearers misunderstood them. Writers, however, must strive to be clear, logical, and fair, or they will be found out.

Good writing goes hand in hand with a sense of human possibility and limitation. Thus historians usually write as if people had the power to choose in the past. The tension between what historical figures did and what they might have done gives history part of its excitement. Herbert Butterfield, a respected philosopher of history, wrote that "history deals with the drama of human life as the affair of individual personalities, possessing self-consciousness, intellect, and freedom."[3] As drama, every part of the past has a unique quality. Every event we study in history existed in its own network of cause and effect, its own set of relations between people and events, its own modes of thought, usually taken for granted by the societies themselves, often assumed to be a divine ordination that could not be changed. A thunderstorm roars over the Kansas prairie today, and the unflappable television meteorologist explains that the storm is the result of a collision between a cold front and a warm front. In ancient Mesopotamia, the Babylonians heard in the thunder the

---

[3] Herbert Butterfield, *Christianity and History* (New York: Scribner's, 1950), 26.

voice of their god Marduk and thought that he was hurling lightning bolts into the earth. In these and countless other ways, spontaneous responses to many experiences in the past were different from those of the present day. Part of our task as historians is to think our way into the minds of the people who lived in earlier times so we can think about experience as they did.

Yet we can never fully abandon our own perceptions; we cannot recover the past exactly as people then thought of life and the world. Historians must always put something of themselves into the stories they tell; never are they empty vessels through which the records of the past spew forth as if they were an untouched truth about a past. This inevitable insertion of the historian into historical accounts is what J. H. Hexter called an application of "the second record," encompassing "everything which historians bring to their confrontation with the record of the past."[4] While this is an inevitable legacy of the historian's work, it is one that must always be kept in check lest the stories which emerge lose any semblance of credulity. And that is a crucial test: are the stories, as well as the explanations and analysis they offer, credible?

Sometimes credulity undermines historians' assumptions, such as long-standing notions that focused historical accounts almost entirely on what men did. If women entered the story, it was because they did things male historians generally expected men to do. They ruled countries, as did Elizabeth I of England; they refined radium, as did Marie Curie in France; they wrote novels, as did Shikibu Murasaki in eleventh-century Japan. Now historians are turning to many other areas of historical interest. A random glance through recent issues of *The American Historical Review* will show, in addition to Professor Kashani-Sabet's article on Iranian Humanism, discussions such as Catherine Kudlick's review essay on "Disability History: Why We Need Another 'Other.'"[5] And books such as Asunción Lavrin's, *Women, Feminism, and*

---

[4] Hexter, *History Primer*, 79.
[5] Catherine J. Kudlick, "Disability History: Why We Need Another 'Other,'" *The American Historical Review* 108 (2003): 763–793.

Social Change in Argentina, Chile, and Uruguay, 1890–1940,[6] provide insights into the history of feminism. These are topics that conventional male historians of a century ago dismissed as irrelevant, but that today occupy an honored and fascinating place in serious historical research. In a similar way historians such as John Thornton, in his *Africa and Africans in the Making of the Atlantic World, 1400–1680,*[7] study the role of people of African descent in many societies, while still others write of the history of immigrants, labor history, sexual history, and the history of fashion or sport. All these and more demonstrate interests of historians toiling to uncover as much of the human experience as possible and leading the profession of history itself away from the notion that to understand the past we need only understand the personalities and decisions of a few white male leaders.

Whatever its subject, the study of history is an unending detective story. Historians try to solve puzzles in the evidence and to tell a story that will give order to the confusion of data we inherit from the past. Historians make connections, assign causes, trace defects, make comparisons, uncover patterns, locate dead ends, and find influences that continue through the generations until the present. And in doing so they apply their minds to the sources and their considered judgments to the evidence, writing those stories about the past they intend to be both credible and true.

You, too, encounter history by reading, and by your own writing as well. By reading books and articles you slowly gain some understanding of the shape of the past, the general framework within which events took place. When you study history in college, you also write about the past using the methods of professional historians. Writing helps all of us think about what we know, and of course it helps your instructors see what you know and how you think. In your history courses you may be asked to write

---

6 Asunción Lavrin, *Women, Feminism, and Social Change in Argentina, Chile, and Uruguay, 1890–1940* (Lincoln: University of Nebraska Press, 1995).

7 John Thornton, *Africa and Africans in the Making of the Atlantic World, 1400–1680,* 2d ed. (Cambridge: Cambridge University Press, 1998).

brief essays of perhaps only one or two pages, either as homework assignments or during class, frequently reflecting on some assigned reading. Sometimes your writing will take the form of essay answers to questions on exams. Occasionally you might be asked to review a history book, either one that you select or one that is assigned to you. And often you may also be expected to prepare longer papers that will require you to conduct research in your own college library, perhaps on the Internet, and elsewhere as well.

Even though your writing about the past will take a number of forms, some basic principles apply to writing any history essay. Perhaps the most important is that thinking about the past is the key to writing history. Thus, this is a book both about methods of historical study and about methods in writing. It should help you gain some understanding of general problems underlying all historical study, and it should help your writing in all your college or university courses. It should also make you a better detective and a better teller of some of the innumerable stories that taken together make up the study of the past. We will discuss research you can conduct in your own college library or on the Internet and also include a brief section about how to take notes on your reading and research. Our emphasis will be on how to use those notes and your acquired knowledge to do well on research papers, shorter essays, and on examinations you may write in a history course.

BASIC PRINCIPLES FOR HISTORY ESSAYS

Obviously, history is far more than an assembly of facts about what happened in the past. It is the writer's interpretation of facts that raises questions, provokes curiosity, and makes us ask the questions *who, what, where, when,* and *why.* The writer's interpretation should concentrate on a central argument, or *thesis* that binds everything in an essay together. No matter what kind of essay you are writing, once you have developed your thesis that will tie the entire essay together, there are six key principles which can help you in examining your own writing to see if it conforms to the expectations that readers—including your instructors—bring to their reading of history essays. Don't disappoint them. Guide your own writing by the following standards.

1. Good history essays are sharply focused on a limited topic.

You can develop a thrill of historical discovery *only* if your topic is sufficiently limited to let you study and think about the sources carefully. If you are able to choose your own topic, select one you can manage in the time and space you have available; this is true for writing essay test responses as well papers that allow you more time to develop your thoughts. Sometimes your instructor may assign a topic for your essay. Usually, such prescribed topics are already sharply focused, but even if they are not you can usually find ways to limit the essay you prepare.

Historians often use very specific research to explore broader questions, as you can see in Charles Ambler's essay in *The American Historical Review* on "Popular Films and the Colonial Audience: The Movies in Northern Rhodesia." Professor Ambler begins very specifically:

> During the 1940s and 1950s, no visitor to the coppermining cities of the colonial Northern Rhodesia (Zambia) in central Africa could escape the visible marks of the impact of American films. In the vast company compounds that housed the African miners and their families on the Copperbelt, groups of African boys, "dressed in home-made paper 'chaps' and cowboy hats, and carrying crudely carved wooden pistols," were a ubiquitous presence running through the streets and alleys in endless games of cowboys and Indians. Others appeared "more sinister, . . . with a black mask over the eyes and a wooden dagger in the belt." As they engaged in their mock battles, they could be heard shouting, "Jeke, Jeke," a local corruption of "Jack," the universal term among urban moviegoers in the British central African colonies for the heroes of cowboy films. In the same streets, young men affected styles of dress that plainly showed the influence of westerns and gangster films—ten-gallon hats, kerchiefs, and so forth.

> This phenomenon of "Copperbelt Cowboys" and its manifestation in urban areas across much of British-ruled Africa vividly demonstrates the rapid and pervasive penetration of mythic Hollywood screen imagery into even remote corners of the empire.

Professor Ambler, however, is careful in his next paragraph to make certain his readers appreciate that the specific focus of his essay serves a broader historical purpose, since it "takes up the history of film entertainment in Northern Rhodesia in order to explore the broad question of the transmission and reception of Western mass culture in the context of colonialism."[8] This is precisely the sort of technique that you can use to focus your essays. There is a lesson here for any young historian: If you try to do too much, you will not do anything. Often discussing your essays, and especially your longer papers, with your instructor will be a valuable aid in helping you to focus your writing appropriately.

Keeping your focus clear should also lead you to a conclusion which will mirror the points that you made as you began your essay. Once you have introduced the puzzle you wish to consider, you should clearly tell the story that will engage your readers. But writers of history essays should not work toward surprise endings! Inexperienced writers often fall into the temptation to withhold necessary information or otherwise distract readers to prevent them from guessing where the story is going. Such tactics are annoying, and professional historians do not use them. The climax in a history paper is usually a place where the last block of information is fitted in place and the writer's case is proved as well as his or her knowledge permits. The paper closes shortly after the climax because once the case is proved, a summary of the significance of the events or ideas reflecting how the essay began is all that is necessary.

---

8 Charles Ambler, "Popular Films and Colonial Audiences: The Movies in Northern Rhodesia," *The American Historical Review* 106 (2001): 81–82. We have omitted Professor Ambler's citations of his sources.

For example, once Professor Ambler presents the story of cinema and its influence in Northern Rhodesia, he comes to the climax and then quickly finishes by returning to the points he made in the beginning of his essay:

> In postcolonial Zambia, the introduction of television and more recently the proliferation of small video dens and individually owned video-cassette recorders has effectively pushed the bioscope—formal film showings—to the margins of entertainment. The current popularity of martial arts and other contemporary action movies has overshadowed the deep affection for the cowboy genre exhibited by several genera-tions of viewers in the industrial towns of the Copperbelt and elsewhere in east, central, and southern Africa. But if the encounter of African audiences with film in the 1940s and 1950s lacked the complexity of the diverse and fragmented circulation of media that is characteristic of Zambia and the rest of southern Africa today, it is apparent that the critical process through which audiences consume visual media devel-oped on a diet of horse operas.[9]

Of course, coordinating the beginning and end of your essay without careful attention to what comes between will not be suffi-cient to impress your readers. The main quality of any story is that it makes readers relive the experience it describes. A good writer cre-ates the experience of living through events or of living through a step-by-step interpretation of those events. Any good piece of writ-ing leads you through a process of discovery, providing information that lets you follow the writer's lead, finally arriving at the climax where everything comes together. Later on we shall suggest that when you pick up a history book to use in your research, you read the last chapter before you read the entire book. In a good essay or book about history, you can know how the story comes out and still appreciate the art of the historian in getting to that conclusion. Readers not only want to know how things come out but also how they happen.

---

[9] Ambler, "Popular Films and Colonial Audiences," 105.

2. History essays should have a clearly stated argument.

Historians write essays to interpret something they want readers to know about the past. They provide data—information from their sources—and their argument about what the evidence means. Here "argument" here does not mean angry, insulting debate as though anyone who disagrees with you is a fool. Rather, it is the main thing the writer wants to tell readers, the reason for writing the essay. It is the *thesis* of the essay, the proposition that the writer wants readers to accept. A good historical essay quietly expresses the thrill of a writer's discovery. You cannot have that thrill yourself or convey it to others if you do nothing but repeat what others have said about your topic. Don't be content with telling a story others have told hundreds of time, the sort of story you might copy out of an encyclopedia whose aim is to give you nothing but the facts. Find something puzzling in the evidence, and try to solve the puzzle or to explain why it is a puzzle. Ask a question and try to answer it. But get to the point straightaway.

A good essay sets the scene quickly, reveals a tension to be resolved, and sets out in the direction of a solution. Some writers take so long to introduce their essays that readers lose interest before they get to the writer's real beginning. Some writers shovel out piles of background information or long accounts of previous scholarship in a somewhat frantic effort to prove that the writer has studied the issue. Or they may give some sort of moral justification for the topic, implying something like this: "I am writing this paper to make a better world and to prove that I am on the right side." The best writers have something to say and start saying it quickly. Readers should know your general subject in the first paragraph, and by the next paragraph they should usually know why you have written your essay and the argument you wish to make.

Consider the opening paragraphs of Professor Leora Auslander's essay in a recent issue of *The American Historical Review*. She quickly makes clear the problem she sees in the usual practice of historians, and then moves directly to her thesis:

> Historians are, by profession, suspicious of things. Words are our stock-in-trade. This is not to say, of course, that historians have never had recourse to non-linguistic sources. From the use of archaeological evidence in the nineteenth century to Marc Bloch's brilliant notion that the intricacies of medieval landholding patterns could be deciphered by observing the interwar French countryside from a small plane, historians have looked beyond the holdings of archives and libraries. Scholars of the ancient, medieval, and early modern worlds, and of science and technology—those whose written sources are limited or whose very object is material—have pushed the evidentiary boundaries the furthest, although some modernists and social and cultural historians have also used visual, material, and musical sources. Despite these initiatives, however, most historians view words as the most trustworthy as well as the most informative sources; everything else is merely illustrative or supplementary.
>
> I will argue here, by contrast, that expanding the range of our canonical sources will provide better answers to familiar historical questions as well as change the very nature of the questions we are able to pose and the kind of knowledge we are able to acquire about the past. Each form of human expression has its unique attributes and capacities; limiting our evidentiary base to one of them—linguistic—renders us unable to grasp important dimensions of human experience, and our explanations of major historical problems are thereby impoverished. Within the category of the extralinguistic, I will make an argument for the utility and importance of material culture in particular.[10]

Her second paragraph begins with her thesis which she then explains by outlining some of the argument she will make in her essay.

Make careful note of this example. Once you have begun your essay, don't digress. Stick to the point. Be sure everything in your essay serves your main purpose, and be sure your readers understand the

---

[10] Leora Auslander, "Beyond Words," *The American Historical Review,* 110 (2005): 1015.

connection to your main purpose of everything you include. Don't imagine that you have to put everything you know into one essay. An essay makes a point. It is not an excuse to pour out facts as if you were dumping the contents of a can onto a tabletop. As Auslander writes in her conclusion, historians must have a commitment "to the goal of understanding, interpreting, and perhaps even explaining the world beyond the text or the object."[11] And as her essay demonstrates, even as historians look for "extralinguistic" evidence they must *write* clearly about their conclusions.

3. History essays are built, step by step, on carefully acknowledged evidence.

You must also give readers reasons to believe your story. Your readers must accept you as an authority for the essay you present to them. You cannot write history off the top of your head, and you cannot parade your opinions unless you support them. Writing about history is much like proving a case in a court of law. A good lawyer does not stand before a jury and say, "My friends, I firmly believe my client is innocent and so you should as well." The jury will not believe her unless she can produce some evidence. So it is with the historical essay. Your readers are judge and jury. You assume the role of the lawyer in arguing your case. It is all very good if your readers think you are sincere or high-minded or even eloquent. It is much more important that you convince them that you are right. To do that you must command your evidence, present it clearly and carefully, and fully acknowledge where you have found it.

But what is evidence? The issue is complicated. Evidence is detailed factual information from primary and secondary sources. Primary sources are texts nearest to any subject of investigation. Secondary sources are always written *about* primary sources. For example, primary sources for an essay about the Mexican revolutionary Emiliano Zapata early in this century would be letters,

---

11 Auslander, 1045.

speeches, and other writings of Zapata himself, and perhaps also objects he owned or created. Secondary sources would be books and articles by scholars such as John Womack and Samuel Brunk who have made careers of studying Zapata's movement and his assassination. Always keep in mind that good essays and papers are based on primary sources; so for such a topic you would consider not only the works Professors Womack and Brunk, but if at all possible those of Zapata himself.

In writing a research essay, you must sift through all the available sources, both primary and secondary, decide what is reliable and what not, what is useful and what not, and how you will use these sources in your work. And in writing shorter essays, such as those on exams, you must keep in mind what evidence you have learned about and mention it. When you make a generalization, immediately support it by quoting, summarizing, or otherwise referring to a source. Generalizations are unconvincing without the help of specific information to give them content.

Evidence is everywhere. The letters and papers of men and women, famous and obscure, make fascinating records of their times, and many collections of such evidence have been published from the classical age to the present. Letters and journals make fascinating reading, especially if they cover long periods of time, and they are gold mines for the historian. You can pick a subject and follow the writer's thoughts on it, or about events related to the subject, and have an excellent paper for a college history course. Similarly, newspapers (many are preserved in microform or digital formats) often provide exceptional insights into the past which may stimulate your curiosity and help you formulate the sorts of puzzles that make for good historical essays. They may also provide significant details to supplement the other sources available to you.

Sources of local history abound in courthouses, diaries, letters, tax records, city directories, and myriad other records. These sources can provide details, often small ones, which can make the past come alive in a moment. And never forget the power of the interview in writing about history. If you write about any historical event of the past fifty or sixty years, often with a little effort you can find somebody who participated in it. Participants frequently may be delighted to share their stories with you. And their stories can illuminate major social movements in the country as a whole. You may also find transcripts of previous interviews in local history publications, newspapers, or archive collections. But always remember that participants can get things wrong, either in their interviews or in what they might have written about their experiences. Human beings forget, or they tell the story in such a way to exalt themselves, and sometimes they simply lie. The historian is always skeptical enough to check out the stories, even from eyewitnesses. In doing so, you frequently will confirm that secondary sources are also essential. You should always consult books and articles written by historians about the subject you write about yourself. These books and articles will help you learn how to think about history, and they will provide much information that you can use.

Historians and their readers love evidence. They love telling details. They love old things. They immerse themselves in evidence—both primary and secondary sources—see its patterns, and write about them. Trying to write a good history essay without evidence is like trying to ride up a mountain on a bicycle without wheels. So historians fit their evidence together to create a story—an explanation, an argument—and they document their sources by means of footnotes, endnotes, or attributions written into the text. Even as you write, however, remember you will only gain authority for your own work if you demonstrate that you are familiar with *both* the primary sources and the work of others who have studied the same material. But the confidence you develop by providing evidence for your points is only as good as the confidence your readers have in how you obtained it. If you make a careless summary of your evidence or simply or get it wrong, you lose the respect of knowledgeable readers. The recent experience of one historian, Michael Bellesiles, is very instructive for any young historian.

Almost immediately after its publication in 2000, Professor Bellesiles's book, *Arming America: The Origins of a National Gun Culture,* was widely praised and his thesis, that the American "gun culture" was a post–Civil War development, enmeshed him in political arguments with many who believe the importance of gun ownership in America is older than the Constitution. In the midst of that controversy, historians began to examine his use of evidence only to find much to question: inaccurate citations to archival holdings, misreading of documents, generalizations based on limited sampling of court records, and sloppy recording of his data. Although Professor Bellesiles made several statements in his defense, none proved sufficient to quiet the outcry, and trustees of the prestigious Bancroft Prize for historical writing withdrew the award they had originally given to him for the book.[12]

Bellesiles's sad experience should be instructive. Be certain that you take careful note of the sources you consult. It is important that you be clear about what you learned from which source, and that you quote correctly any material you copy directly from those sources. This is true not only for the notes you make from written sources, but also for those you obtain from increasingly widely available electronic resources. Both require special care.

While documenting your sources is very important in historical writing, it is widely accepted that you do not have to document matters of common knowledge. Martin Luther was born on November 10, 1483. The Japanese attacked Pearl Harbor in Hawaii on Sunday morning, December 7, 1941. Zora Neale Hurston wrote the novel *Their Eyes Were Watching God*. Pieces of information such as these are common knowledge. They are not disputed, are known to anyone who knows anything about these subjects, and can easily be verified. You may find that some ideas you get on your own about such subjects are not precisely the same as those you read in secondary sources. You should then document those secondary sources and, either in a footnote or in the body of your text, point out the similarities and the differences between those sources and what you have written.

---

[12] Several perspectives on this controversy may be found in a "*Forum: Historians and Guns,*" *William and Mary Quarterly,* 59 (2002): 203–268.

4. History essays must represent your own original work.

Plagiarism—presenting the thoughts or words of others as your own—is the ultimate dishonesty in writing. In recent years, several well known historians, including Doris Kearns Goodwin and the late Stephen Ambrose, have been forced to admit that due to their personal inattention, portions of several of their books were copied from the work of other writers. Claims of simple carelessness or exuberance in telling a story, such as those made by Professor Ambrose, are simply insufficient. Readers naturally expected better from him, and they will of you as well. Frequently authors who are challenged in court by those whose work they have appropriated and presented as their own face costly and embarrassing results. And in any case, such thefts of intellectual property are seldom forgotten.

The case of Alex Haley is a famous example. Haley claimed that his book *Roots* came from his investigation into the history of his own ancestors who came as slaves from Africa. The book was made into a television miniseries that gripped millions of Americans when it was aired over twelve nights in 1977; its success also seemed to reinvigorate the study of African American history throughout the United States. Haley, however, was charged with plagiarism and paid $650,000 in civil damages to the writer whose work he had copied. Further investigations by historians revealed that he had made up much of his evidence, and when he died in 1992, his reputation among scholars was in ruins. Leading historians usually dismiss his work, and even the small memorial to Haley in Knoxville, Tennessee—near his hometown—ignores any claims he might have been a historian. Instead, an inscription describes him only as a "journalist and novelist who shaped the contemporary African American consciousness." His sad example, and that of other historians since, should be a warning to all writers: acknowledge and document your sources with care!

Your efforts to avoid plagiarism should begin even as you are taking notes from your sources. Take special care to record most of your notes in your own words. And *always* put material you copy directly from your sources in quotation marks in your notes. If you later use that information word for word in your essay as you found it in the sources—even if it is only a short phrase or brief sentence—put it in quotation marks in your essay as well, and make a clear citation to the source you are quoting. Also keep in mind that no matter how you keep notes, electronic research and writing advances come with associated dangers. In particular, the ease of "block and click" operations used to capture and move electronic text from one file (or even a Web page) to another can be a temptation for including large segments of a source directly in your notes. If you use this technique, be certain to use quotation marks and also mark those notes as quotations. Failing to do so could lead to careless copying of some material directly into your essay where it might appear as if it were your own work. If you are careless, you will be guilty of plagiarism. Remember: it is *your* responsibility to avoid such errors.

Lest you slip into careless habits in using electronic—or any other—sources, you should be aware of the greatly increased use of Turnitin and similar services which allow you and your instructors to check the originality of your essays. Some colleges and universities use the service as a matter of campus policy, but it is also available for use by individual instructors. Even if you do not submit your essay through a Turnitin interface, your papers may be submitted directly by your instructor. Your work will be compared with most of the public Internet content, many subscription based content providers (including writing for payment sites), as well as previous papers submitted to Turnitin. And there is also a considerable database of print sources used in making the comparisons as well. Reports on these comparisons—including side by side contrasts with the originals—are generated for your instructors and sometimes for you as well. Thus, Turnitin provides a resource for the speedy checking of your work for originality. Understanding the availability of such a service should serve as an encouragement for your careful efforts at original writing.

Our best advice is that to avoid being charged with plagiarism you should always make certain that your essays are your own work and that you always give credit for ideas you get from someone else, even if you paraphrase or express those ideas in your own words. Take the advice of Professor Peter Hoffer to paraphrase only "with great care . . . to avoid falling into plagiarism":

> Paraphrasing lends itself to a wide range of errors. In particular, a paraphrase . . . [made] in the course of research, may be mistaken by the author for his or her own idea or language and reappear in the author's piece without any attribution. Mosaic paraphrases patching together quotations from a variety of secondary sources, and close paraphrases, wherein the author changes a word or two and reuses a passage from another author without quotations marks, also constitute plagiarism.
>
> In print, all paraphrases, no matter how long or how many works are paraphrased, must be followed by citations to the sources that are as clear and precise as those provided for a direct quotation.[13]

The process of paraphrasing and summarizing, however, is sometimes hard to grasp. The following example may help you see how to do so in your own research and writing, thus avoiding the problem of plagiarism. Here is a paragraph from a recent book by world historian Jerry Bentley:

> Beginning in the fifteenth century, and continuing to some extent to the present day, new configurations of technology and new patterns of disease favored Europeans in their dealings with nonwestern peoples. The technology in question was not absolutely new, nor was it always European in origin. Much of it traced ultimately to Tang and Song inventions: gunpowder, the compass, the stern-post rudder, and other elements of nautical technology all came ultimately from China. Other items also came from eastern parts, most notably the lanteen sail, which originated in the Indian Ocean and came to the Mediterranean through the agency of Arab merchants and mariners. The Europeans borrowed much of their naval and military technology, but they refined, accumulated, and combined it to the point that they at least matched and most often exceeded the technological development of other peoples. When the Europeans ventured into the Atlantic Ocean in the

---

13 Peter Charles Hoffer, "Reflections on Plagiarism—Part 1: 'A Guide for the Perplexed,'" *Perspectives: Newsmagazine of the American Historical Association*, 42, 2 (February 2004): 19.

fifteenth century, they not only possessed highly maneuverable vessels and the instruments necessary to chart their courses (at least approximately) and return safely but also drew upon an arsenal of powerful weapons that dismembered and profoundly disoriented people who had not before encountered such destructive machinery. Sophisticated naval and military technologies by no means provided Europeans with the means to dominate all the peoples they encountered—certainly not before the development of the steamboat and advanced weapons in the nineteenth century—but they underwrote western hegemony in the world over a very long term.[14]

And here is a way you might summarize this passage, using your own words as you might when paraphrasing:

> Jerry Bentley makes a strong case that European imperialism rested on technology. Most of the key inventions, in military and naval equipment, were borrowed and then both modified and enhanced by European craftsmen. These developments gave them a clear advantage over other peoples they encountered and then conquered.

These ideas clearly come from Bentley's book, even though you do not directly quote him. In making such a summary you *must* make a citation to Bentley's work saying, in effect, "This is where I got these ideas." Citations of this sort will usually be much more common in your essays than ones documenting a direct quotation. That is, you will paraphrase or summarize much more frequently than you quote directly. Be certain that you do so with care!

While the issue of plagiarism may seem little more than a theoretical or moral dilemma facing a writer of history, it is a serious matter in practice. Keep in mind that at colleges and universities the penalties for plagiarism are severe. In many universities plagiarists are summoned before a disciplinary board, and sometimes expelled

---

[14] Jerry H. Bentley, *Old World Encounters* (New York: Oxford University Press, 1993), 183.

for one or more terms of study, and the plagiarism usually is recorded permanently on their academic records.

5. History essays reflect the dispassionate thoughts of the author.

While you should take great care to acknowledge what previous historians have written about a topic, do not disappoint your readers by telling them only what other people have said about your subject. Try to show them that by reading your work, they will learn something new or see old knowledge in a new light, one that you have shed on the subject by your own study and thinking.

One of the saddest things we have found about teaching is the conviction of too many of our students that they have nothing fresh and interesting to say about their topics. They don't trust themselves. They cannot express a thought unless they have read it somewhere else. One reason for this lack of confidence is that some students insist on writing about large, general topics that other people have written about hundreds of times. Only a little searching in almost any college or university library will turn up evidence of topics that have seldom been written about. If you take the time to look, you too can turn up new information and shape history essays with new and original insights.

You may not find new facts, but you can think carefully about the facts at your disposal and come up with something fresh and interesting. You can see new relationships. You can see causes and effects and connections that others have missed. You may reflect on motives and influences. You may spot places where some sources are silent. You can present your own conclusions, based on the evidence you have accumulated, which have the weight of authority behind them.

Some students go to the library looking for information on a broad subject like the beginnings of the Civil War and take a piece of information here and another piece there. They stick it all together without contributing anything of their own except manual dexterity. They retell a story that has been told thousands of times, and they do not present a thought that they have not read elsewhere. Why not instead read the speech Senator Jefferson Davis of Mississippi made in the United States Senate as he resigned to become president of the Confederacy? You might explain in an essay his justification for secession—and see if you think he left something out. Then you have a thoughtful paper. Do not be happy until you shape a story that cannot be read in any encyclopedia or textbook in the field.

Offering your own original ideas does not mean that you should choke your prose with your own emotions. Historians identify with the people and the times they write about, and often in studying history emotions are aroused. In writing about the past, you judge people and decide whether they were good or bad. The best way to convey these judgments is to tell what these people did or said. You don't have to prove that you are on the side of the angels. You should trust your readers. If characters you describe did terrible things, readers can see the evil if you give them the details. If characters did noble things, your readers can tell that, too, without any emotional insistence on your part.

Describing the British retreat from Concord and Lexington on April 19, 1775, historian Louis Birnbaum simply narrates the story:

> The mood of the British soldiers was murderous. They surged around houses along the route, instantly killing anyone found inside. Some of the regulars looted whatever they could find, and some were killed while looting by Minutemen who had concealed themselves in the houses. Houses with fires in the hearth were burned down simply by spreading the embers about. Generally, those homes without fires on the hearth escaped destruction because it was too time-consuming to start a fire with steel and flint. As the column approached Menotomy, the 23rd Regiment was relieved of rear-guard duty by the marine battalion. Colonial fire reached a bloody crescendo in Menotomy, and again British troops rushed house after house, killing everyone found inside, including an invalid named Jason Russell.[15]

---

[15] Louis Bimbaum, *Red Dawn at Lexington* (Boston: Houghton Mifflin, 1986), 184.

The author could have said, "The criminal and bloodthirsty British soldiers acted horribly in what they did to those poor, innocent people, and those wicked British soldiers killed in the act of looting houses got what they deserved." But readers don't need such coercive comments, and they often resent them. If you present the details, you can trust your readers to have the reactions you expect. You waste time and seem a little foolish if you preach at them.

Good historians try to tell the truth about what happened. If you study any issue long enough and carefully enough, you will form opinions about it. You will think you know why something happened, or you will suppose that you understand someone. And you may develop strong personal views about the personalities or the outcome. Yet the evidence in history seldom stacks up entirely on one side of an issue, especially in the more interesting problems about the past. Different parts of the evidence can often contradict each other; using your own judgment about it all means that you must face such contradictions squarely. If you do not, knowledgeable readers may decide that you are careless, incompetent, or even dishonest. History is not a seamless garment. Knowledge of the past—or of almost anything else—has bumps and rips and blank spots that remain even when historians have done their best to put together a coherent account of it.

It is also true that different historians interpret the same data in different ways. So it is not unusual to find new and different interpretations of the past, sometimes including new evidence and sometimes rethinking what the well-known evidence means. This *revisionism* is hardly the dangerous approach to the past that is occasionally denounced in the press; rather, it is the normal work of writing history. Joyce Appleby, Lynn Hunt, and Margaret Jacob—the first two elected presidents of the American Historical Association—have noted that historians "do not so much revise historical knowledge as they reinvest it with contemporary interest."[16] But they do so with

---

[16] Joyce Appleby, Lynn Hunt, and Margaret Jacob, *Telling the Truth About History* (New York: W. W. Norton, 1994), 265.

care and consideration of other points of view. Consider this opening paragraph by Camilla Townsend in her recent *American Historical Review* article, "Burying the White Gods: New Perspectives on the Conquest of Mexico":

> In 1552, Francisco López de Gómara, who had been chaplain and secretary to Hernando Cortés while he lived out his old age in Spain, published an account of the conquest of Mexico. López de Gómara himself had never been to the New World, but he could envision it nonetheless. "Many [Indians] came to gape at the strange men, now so famous, and at their attire, arms and horses, and they said, 'These men are gods!'" The chaplain was one of the first to claim in print that the Mexicans had believed the conquistadors to be divine. Among the welter of statements made in the Old World about the inhabitants of the New, this one found particular resonance. It was repeated with enthusiasm, and soon a specific version gained credence: the Mexicans had apparently believed in a god named Quetzalcoatl, who long ago had disappeared in the east, promising to return from that direction on a certain date. In an extraordinary coincidence, Cortés appeared off the coast in that very year and was mistaken for Quetzalcoatl by the devout Indians. Today, most educated persons in the United States, Europe, and Latin America are fully versed in this account, as readers of this piece can undoubtedly affirm. In fact, however, there is little evidence that the indigenous people ever seriously believed the newcomers were gods, and there is no meaningful evidence that any story about Quetzalcoatl's return from the east ever existed before the conquest. A number of scholars of early Mexico are aware of this, but few others are. The cherished narrative is alive and well, and in urgent need of critical attention.[17]

Professor Townsend's approach illustrates the very reasonable way historians bring new ideas of their own into an essay. You can do the same. You do not weaken your argument by recognizing different views. On the contrary, you strengthen your case by showing readers that you know what others have said, even if their opinions contradict your own. Readers will believe you if you deal with

---

[17] Camila Townsend, "Burying the White Gods: New Perspectives on the Conquest of Mexico," *The American Historical Review* 108 (2003): 659.

contrary opinions honestly, but they will scorn your work if you pretend that contradictions don't exist. This advice translates into a simple principle: Be honest, not arrogant. Nothing turns readers off so quickly as to suppose that the writer is not being fair.

6. History essays are clearly written with an intended audience in mind.

Readers are also turned off if they are distracted by asking questions like these as they read: "Is that word spelled correctly?" "Why is a comma missing here?" "Does this word fit the context?" Reading—like writing—is hard work, especially when the material is dense or complicated, as it often is in history courses. Readers want to pay attention to what a writer says. A careless attitude towards the conventions—among them common practices of grammar and punctuation—may not bother writers because they think they know what they want to say. But it throws readers off.

Students who complain when instructors enforce the conventions do themselves a great disservice. In the world beyond college, few things about your writing will be more harshly judged than careless disregard for the conventions. Most everyone would like to believe their ideas are so compelling that no one can resist them, no matter how sloppily they write. Readers you seek to impress in a job application, a report, or a letter will judge otherwise. But merely reading over our suggestions, or listening to others from your instructors, is not enough. You must actively apply them and others, such as those in Bryan A. Garner's excellent essay in the new, fifteenth edition of *The Chicago Manual of Style*.[18]

In part, this means you should respect the audience for whom you are writing. Different essays are intended for different audiences; always consider what your intended audience already knows. Just as you convey to your readers an "implied author" in what you write,

---

[18] Bryan A. Garner, "Grammar and Usage," in *The Chicago Manual of Style*, 15th ed., 145–237 (Chicago: University of Chicago Press, 2003).

you should also write with an implied reader in mind, someone you think may read your work. For most history courses, you should write for your instructor and other students who are interested in your topic but may not be specialists in the field. Define important terms. Give enough information to provide a context for your essay. Say something about your sources, but do not get lost in background information that your readers know already. The best you can do is to imagine yourself as a reader and consider the sort of thing you might read and believe, and write accordingly.

It is not always an easy task. The main principle is that you must always be making decisions about what you need to tell your readers and what you think they know already. For example, if you write an interpretation of Martin Luther King Jr.'s *Letter from Birmingham Jail* of 1965, you will bore readers and even offend them if you write as if they have never heard of Dr. King. In the same way, you don't inform your readers that Shakespeare was an English playwright or that Nelson Mandela was the first black president of South Africa.

We tell our students that they should write their essays so that if a friend or spouse picked one up, they could read it with the same understanding and pleasure they might find in an article in a serious magazine. The essay should be complete in itself. The important terms should be defined. Everyone quoted or mentioned in the essay should be identified—unless someone is well known to the general public. All the necessary information should be included. Try to imagine a friend picking up an essay and not being able to stop until he or she has finished the piece. And it is always a good idea to have some other person read your work and try to say back to you what he or she thinks you have said; they might also be able to suggest improvements in your writing!

Having someone read your essay and make comments on it, however, does not change your own responsibility for proofreading your essay carefully. Read it over and over to find misspelled words, lapses in grammar, typos, and places where you have inadvertently left out a word (a common error in these days of writing with the computer). Use the spell-checker (and grammar-checker) on your word-processing program. But remember! The computer cannot replace the brain, although it will often help you ask questions about your writing before your readers do.

These principles for a good essay should serve you well. Keep them in mind as you write your own history essays. This summary checklist below will help you focus on them as you do.

Writer's Checklist

_____ ✔ Have I narrowed my topic sufficiently?

_____ ✔ Do the first and last sections of my essay mirror each other?

_____ ✔ Do I have a clearly stated argument?

_____ ✔ Are my own ideas on the subject clear?

_____ ✔ Is the evidence on which I based my essay clear?

_____ ✔ Is the essay my own, original work?

_____ ✔ Are my paraphrases in my own words?

_____ ✔ Have I documented my sources?

_____ ✔ Have I written dispassionately?

_____ ✔ Have I acknowledged other views?

_____ ✔ Have I written clearly, using common conventions of written English?

_____ ✔ Have I kept my intended audience in mind?

THINKING ABOUT HISTORY

■ ■ ■

Writing history involves a special way of thinking because the past in all its complexity cannot be recaptured like an instant replay. Real life has no instant replay; history does not repeat itself. The stuff of history—human experience—moves ceaselessly, changing endlessly in a process so complicated that it is like a turning kaleidoscope that never makes the same pattern twice. Consequently, knowing history is only possible through the stories that are told about it, stories that are told by many people, supported by many different kinds of evidence, told in different ways in different times and in different places. Historical research and historical thinking always involve listening to a multitude of voices, mute perhaps on the page but speaking through human intellect as historians try to sort them all out and arrive at the story that is most plausible.

A consciousness of history begins with the knowledge that present and past are different. The writing of history flourished when people fully realized that times were changing, that the new was replacing the old, and the stories of the old should be written down before they were lost. Very soon historians understood as well that to write history means to make an effort to tell the story of the past in language that makes sense to readers in the present, an effort that may distort the story. Yet it is necessary because the past has such power. Human beings want to know how things got this way. They yearn to understand origins and purposes, and essential parts of their own lives in the present are influenced by their understanding of the past.

Not long ago debate was raised anew about the origin of an explosion that sank the U.S. battleship Maine in Cuba's Havana Harbor on February 15, 1898. Shortly after the event, American newspaper reports stirred public opinion to believe that almost 200 American sailors were lost when the Maine was sunk by a bomb planted against its hull by Spanish agents. Not long afterwards the United States declared war against Spain. American troops defeated the Spaniards in Cuba, Puerto Rico, the Philippines, and other territories, and the United States acquired an overseas empire for the first time. Now some evidence seems to suggest that a fire in a coal bunker in the ship itself ignited ammunition stored nearby, sinking the ship. Historical research into the origins of that now distant war serves to make many people cautious when the government tells citizens today that the nation must go to war because its honor or morals are in peril if it does not. Present and past work together to condition attitudes toward both of them.

What *really* happened? That is the fundamental question everyone would like to know about the past. But the problems of history resemble the problems of memory. What were you doing a year ago today? If you keep an appointment book, you can find in it the names of people you saw that day. But what did you say to each other? The journal does not tell you everything. Someone might say to you, "I remember when we sat on the beach at Pawley's Island, South Carolina, year before last in August and talked about Elvis Presley's death." "Oh," you may reply, "I thought that was three years ago in a cafe in Charleston." You may have recorded the conversation in your journal; or you may have forgotten to make an entry that day. So where did the conversation take place? You have sources to check your own memories, as do historians. But like your own sources, the ones historians look to may not provide immediate answers to every puzzle.

The sources for history have been conditioned by when they were created and are also conditioned in the present by how they are read. For example, legends of the saints told in the Middle Ages are filled with miraculous happenings. Saint Denis was said to have been beheaded in Paris while preaching to the pagan Gauls. Legend has it he walked with his head in his hands to the site that later became the monastery of Saint Denis outside the city, and he set his head down there to mark the place where he should be buried. The kings of France were later buried in the monastery church built on the site. A statue of the saint, holding his head in his hands, stands now on the front of Notre Dame Cathedral in Paris, a reconstruction of a statue torn down by mobs during the French Revolution.

Most of us don't believe that people walk about holding their severed heads in their hands, yet you can respect this tale as a charming legend, not literal truth. Did the people of medieval Paris believe the story of the miracle? In a supremely reasonable attitude toward the past, you may assume that the story of Saint Denis was a good way for the bishops of Paris to emphasize the importance of their city and the truth of the orthodox Christian theology they professed. Paris achieved a sacred status because of the miracle. But who can tell? Maybe the medieval bishops *did* believe the story! And perhaps you may have to revise your nice, reasonable explanations for its origins.

The stories historians tell are about human beings living in particular times and places. Human motives are in every age complex, mysterious, and often absurd. Many people in every land do crazy and destructive things for what seems to be no reason, and scapegoats for national calamities or imagined enemies are summoned up by hysterical leaders to be blamed and to have horror inflicted upon them. "Rational" people cannot believe Saint Denis walked across Paris carrying his severed head in his hands. But how could "rational" people also acquiesce in the systematic slaughter of their supposed enemies, as in Armenia at the beginning of the twentieth century or in Rwanda nearer its end?

All this is to say that history involves you in modes of thought common to daily life as well as in the effort to understand acts and ideas utterly foreign to your own. You must weigh evidence, deciding what to believe and what not, what you know and what you think is probable or at least plausible. As historians tell stories about what happened, they try to discover what it all means—and in so doing try to understand better what it is to be a human being. You will begin to think creatively in the study and writing of history by questioning your sources.

QUESTIONING SOURCES

Good history essays are built on primary sources, but secondary sources are also essential to the historian's task, and you should always use them. The trick is not to follow slavishly the materials you find in any of your sources. Use them to add to your own knowledge and to help you shape your own questions about the past. As you read, keep these familiar questions in mind—*who, what, when, where,* and *why*—as your guide; try to answer them briefly as you read. They will help you sort things out and organize your approach to the topic you are writing about.

These questions correspond to an almost universal way that literate people respond to information, and they have long been used by historians in working with sources. When they focus on something that happened, historians ask who the people involved were, what exactly happened, when it happened, where, and why. The answers often overlap. To explain *what* happened is sometimes to explain *why* it happened. And you can scarcely separate a *who* question from a *what* question, because to write about someone is to discuss what that person did.

The overlap of questions is the very reason they are so useful in research. A complex event is like an elaborate tapestry tightly woven of many different-colored threads. The threads are distinct, but they are hard to sort out. These questions help keep your eyes on this or that important thread so you can see how it contributes to the whole. They will help immeasurably in analyzing human actions. The emphasis you place on one question or another may determine the approach you take to writing an essay about a historical event. And thus the focus of your questioning may alter the problems you identify and the story you will tell. Remember, too, that there is not just one *who* question or one *what* question or one *why* question. There may be dozens. Ask as many of them as you can. Push your mind.

These research questions can frequently help you work through the malady referred to as writer's block. All writers experience this affliction at one time or another. You cannot seem to get started writing, cannot go on, or cannot finish. When this happens, it is important to find a place to make a start, even if it is only a small step. Try writing out each of the questions about your topic that occurs to you; don't worry if they seem to overlap. Then try writing various answers to each of them. Often you can give your mind a push by writing out almost anything that comes to mind. Even a nonsense poem, composed out of your frustrations, may help to inspire you to further writing. Certainly, writing stimulates the mind; we cannot emphasize that point enough. Almost any process that makes you write about your topic will fill your mind with thoughts you could not have had if you had not started writing first. Sometimes the rigid discipline of spending ten minutes each day writing a journal entry about your efforts—even if they have not produced anything else that day—can start you on further writing sooner rather than postponing your efforts until later. Or perhaps you can enlist a friend in an electronic chat about your efforts at a regular time each day as another means to jump-start your writing. But above all, don't retreat from your questioning without making *some* effort to write down *something* about your questions and, if you can, what answers you have begun to find.

"*Who*" Questions

Many historical topics center on individuals. If your topic is one of these, you will want to begin with who questions. Who was Pearl Buck? Whom did she write about? Who loved her work? Who were some of her critics? Who was influential in interpreting her work?

As you ask such questions while reading your sources, keep a record of them and jot down the answers—or note that you don't know the answers. You should also recognize a multitude of other questions which occur as you do this. Where did she live in China? What did her missionary experience there contribute to her view of that country? What did she do to influence American attitudes toward China? Why did she win the Nobel Prize? When was the prize given to her? What did literary critics say about her work? What did her fans say about her? What do people say about her work now? When did the attitude about her work begin to change? Why did it change? All these questions will take you to still other sources.

As you ask—and attempt to answer—these additional questions, your thought evolves. You begin to see relations between some of your questions. For example, you may push yourself to ask a dozen or more *where* questions or a multitude of *why* questions. And you may begin to read some of your sources differently. For example, you likely know that American public opinion was shocked when the Communists under Mao Zedong took over the Chinese mainland in 1949. Many politicians, including Senator Joseph McCarthy of Wisconsin, claimed that the United States had "lost" China for democracy because the U.S. Department of State was infested with Communist agents. Did Pearl Buck's idealistic books about China, especially her classic *The Good Earth,* help create an unreal impression of the situation there? Questions such as these can lead you to read—or perhaps reread—Buck's books, reviews of her work written in her own time, and articles written about her since. From them you can find your way to a good essay. And your initial *who* questions will have opened the door to your essay.

"What" Questions

What questions, of course, have their basis in the fundamental problem for historical understanding: What happened? But as you probe your sources, asking *what* questions may involve weeding out legends and misunderstandings to see what really happened. A frequent question that will come to mind as you read your sources is, "What does this mean?" Often you will be trying to see what people in the past meant by the words they used. These meanings can confuse us because they often change.

In the nineteenth century the word "liberal" was used to describe businessmen who wanted to make a place for themselves in a country ruled by an aristocracy with its power based on land. The liberals were capitalists who thought government ought to keep its hands off business. Most liberals believed that the economy ran by implacable laws of supply and demand and that any effort to help working people interfered with those laws and was bound to lead to catastrophe.

In the twentieth century, the word "liberal" was used by Americans to describe those who wanted government to hold the balance of power between the strong and the weak, the rich and the poor. At the beginning of the twenty-first century neither major American political party wants to use the word because it implies spending by the government for programs to help the poor and the weak, and consequent taxes to support that spending. In some political rhetoric "the 'L' word" has become a special category for scorn.

What relations exist between the use of the words in these different ways? Liberals in both the nineteenth and twentieth centuries advocated "liberty," the root word of "liberal." Nineteenth-century liberals wanted to create liberty for the business classes who suffered under customs that gave political power to landed aristocrats. Twentieth-century liberals tried to create more liberty for the poor, including the liberty to have a public school education with its recognition of talent and opportunities for advancement. What changed in American life to account for the difference in the concept of liberty? And what brought about the shift in attitudes toward the words "liberal" and "liberalism"?

When you use such broad terms in your writing, you must define what you mean by them. Be on guard against reading today's definition into yesterday's words. Do not rely on simple dictionary definitions; look for the origins of the words and their etymologies, including examples of how they have been used over time. Words are defined by their historical context in time and place, and you must be sure to understand what they originally meant and how that has changed.

In answering *what* questions, historians sometimes try to distinguish between the unique qualities in events and the qualities that seem to repeat themselves. For example, What qualities helped some large states endure for long periods of time? What qualities have seemed to doom others to fall? The questions are fascinating, but the answers are uncertain. One historian may see a pattern of repetition; another may see, in the same events, circumstances unique to a specific time and place. Some Greek and Roman historians believed that history involved cycles of repetition and that to know the past allowed people to predict the future. Few modern historians would make such claims. Some broad patterns repeat themselves. Empires, countries, and cultures rise and fall. To some scholars, these repetitions make it seem that all history is locked into invariable cycles. Viewing history in this way, though, suggests a treadmill on which human beings toil endlessly without getting anywhere. And it can limit the historian's capacity to discover what really happened.

"When" Questions

Sometimes you know exactly when something happened: the moment the first Japanese bombs fell on Pearl Harbor, the day Franklin Roosevelt died, and exactly when the Confederate charge reached its high-water mark on the third day of the battle of Gettysburg. Of course, this certainty is born of our acceptance of a common system of measuring time. Historians know this has not always been the case, and to some extent it is not the case today. The Islamic method of reckoning time, for example, is based on different initial assumptions—the *hijrah* (or flight) of Muhammad from Mecca to Medina, rather than the birth of Jesus—and a different method— lunar rather than solar—of calculating the passage of days. The history of calendars is itself a fascinating subject of historical study. Nonetheless, historians generally accept the western, or Gregorian, method of time calculation to avoid confusion, and it has been a practical and realistic way to answer many *when* questions.

But asking when something happened in relation to something else can provide a fascinating topic of research. When did volcanic eruptions destroy Minoan civilization on Crete? The question is related to the rise of power on the Greek mainland under states such as Athens and Sparta. When did Richard Nixon first learn that members of his White House staff were involved in the now infamous Watergate burglary of June 17, 1972? "When did you know" became an important question put to Nixon and his aides in the subsequent investigations. That question has come to epitomize a skeptical approach to historical sources. And it is one you would do well to adopt in your research and in answering all of these essential questions.

"Where" Questions

Questions about where things happened can often be absorbing. No one knows the exact location of the Rubicon River. Julius Caesar crossed it with his army in violation of a law of the Roman Republic that forbade the army to approach near the capital. But wherever it was, it has another name today. The Rubicon was in northern Italy and formed the border between the Roman province known as Cisalpine Gaul and the Roman Republic itself. But which modern Italian river was then called the Rubicon is a matter of dispute. However, deciding where the Rubicon was might help historians understand how much warning the Roman Senate had when Caesar moved with his troops on the capital.

Where questions involve geography, and you should think about geography when you write. Geography may not yield anything special for your work, but if you ask the right questions, geography may open a door in your mind onto a hitherto unimagined landscape of events and explanation. The Annales school of historical study in France made geography one of its fundamental concerns, asking such questions as how long it took to travel from one place to another in Europe, where the major trade routes were, where different crops were grown, and what cities had the closest relations to one another. For all historians, a good topographical map showing roads, rivers, mountains, passes, coasts, and location of towns remains an indispensable resource. Using such a map, you will be able to ask better questions about your sources.

"Why" Questions

Sometimes you know what happened. But basic curiosity should lead you to ask *why* did it happen: Why did it have the influence it did? These questions—essentially about cause and effect—create an eternal fascination. But cause and effect are like unruly twins. In historical study they are inseparable, yet it is often difficult to see just how they relate to each other. You might call the precipitating, or triggering, cause the one that sets events in motion. The background causes are those that build up and create the context within which the precipitating cause works. Precipitating causes are often dramatic and fairly clear. Background causes are more difficult to sort out and often ambiguous.

The precipitating cause of the American Civil War was the bombardment and capture of Fort Sumter by the forces of South Carolina on April 12, 1861. No one would claim that the incident in Charleston Harbor all by itself caused the Civil War. Behind the events of that Friday morning were many complex differences between North and South. These were background causes of the war, and historians ever since have been trying to sort them all out to tell a sensible and precise story to explain why America's bloodiest war came.

Background causes offer rich possibilities for writing about the *why* of history. They allow writers opportunities for research, analysis, inference, and even conjecture. But precipitating or triggering causes can be worthwhile subjects in themselves. Exactly what happened at Fort Sumter on that April day in 1861? Why were passions so aroused on that particular day in that particular year? The *what* question and the *why* question come together—as they often do.

Good historical writing considers how many different but related influences work on what happens and sees things in context—often a large context of people and events. Nineteenth-century historians thought that if they understood the leaders, they knew everything they needed to know about why historical events happened as they did. But thinking in context means you try to sort out and weigh the relative importance of various causes when you consider any important happening. As a result, more historians are now asking questions such as, Why did a rebellion of Indian soldiers in the service of the East India Company in 1857 in Bengal lead to massacres of British settlers all over India? Why were the British able to persuade other Indians to unite with them in committing horrifying atrocities to put down the rebellion? Such questions lead to investigations into the lives of people often scarcely literate who have left few written records behind. Since it is hard to resurrect the life of the masses, the problem of answering the *why* questions of history becomes complex, sometimes uncertain, yet very fascinating.

Some *why* questions may seem to have been answered more definitively. Yet an inquiring historian may reexamine the original puzzle and find another possible answer that contradicts accepted wisdom. Realizing the potential of this process—known as *revisionism*—should be motivation enough for caution in accepting uncritically what may seem to be settled historical truth. Such skepticism is an essential part of writing history. Asking questions that may have been overlooked, thinking about accepted answers in new ways, carefully reexamining the evidence, and discovering previously unexamined sources, may all turn up new possibilities for retelling a story about the past. Yet this process does require care to ensure that you avoid the many common fallacies that often creep into historical writing.

HISTORICAL FALLACIES

"A fallacy is not merely an error itself," historian David Hackett Fischer observed a number of years ago, "but a way of falling into error. It consists in false reasoning, often from true factual premises, so that false conclusions are generated."[1] In his book on the subject, Professor Fischer suggested quite a number of specific fallacies— and offered examples of each from historical writing. For several years after his book appeared, historians scanned its pages hoping not to find their names included! Far better, though, simply to keep a few of the most common errors in mind so that you might avoid them in your writing.

One of these—the fallacy of the single cause—sometimes emerges out of the difficulties in finding answers to complex *why* questions. A particular possibility may seem to be especially attractive, but it is almost always a mistake to lay too much responsibility for any happening on only one cause. Do not be tempted to give easy and simple causes for complex and difficult problems. For example, do not argue that the Roman Empire fell only because Romans drank water from lead pipes or that the South lost the Civil War only because Lee was defeated at Gettysburg. These events were caused by complex influences, and you should take care to acknowledge those complexities.

By all means you should also avoid the fallacy that comes wearing an elaborate Latin name—*post hoc, ergo propter hoc,* "after this, therefore because of this." It refers to the fallacy of believing that if something happens after something else, the first happening caused the second. A more subtle problem with this fallacy arises with events that are closely related, although one does not necessarily cause the other. The New York stock market crashed in October 1929; the Great Depression followed. But it is a mistake to say that

---

[1] David Hackett Fischer, *Historians' Fallacies: Toward a Logic of Historical Thought* (New York: Harper and Row, 1970), xvii.

the crash caused the Depression; both seem to have been caused by the same economic forces. When you confront this sort of relationship of events in writing essays, you must carefully think out the various strands of causation and avoid making things too simple.

In a similar fallacy of oversimplification, many nineteenth-century historians believed that history was the story of inevitable progress, culminating in a predictable conclusion, such as the triumph of the white races because of their supposed superiority over people of color throughout the world. They viewed this as a step forward, making the entire world better as a result. Other historians have seen history moving according to God's will: when people do good, they thrive; when they violate the laws of God, they decline and suffer. But on close investigation, the swirls and waves of the historical process don't appear to move in such easily predictable patterns.

Similarly, those who assume that learning about the past will allow them to avoid mistakes in the future underestimate the continuous flow of the "new" into human events. New inventions, new ways of thinking, or new combinations of ideas can upset all predictions. Most modern historians understand the need to be cautious in suggesting what history can tell us of both the present and the future. For one thing, they no longer predict inevitable progress in human affairs. It is possible to know history well and still be startled by events. In recent decades, thousands of historians young and old studied the history of the Soviet Union. The U.S. Central Intelligence Agency employed historians to help our government understand how to deal with the Soviet Union and predict what it might do. Yet not one of these scholars predicted anything like the sudden collapse and breakup of the entire Soviet empire in 1989 and 1990.

You may also be familiar with another common fallacy associated with the term "straw man." People set up straw men when they argue against positions their opponents have not taken or when, without evidence, they attribute bad motives to opponents. In response to the idea that the sixteenth century in Europe was marked by much skepticism in matters of religion, an opponent might counter that the sixteenth century could not have experienced religious skepticism because the scientific worldview of Galileo and Newton was unknown—as if religious skepticism depended on a scientific worldview. Such an argument is simply beside the point. Worse, an opponent might advance an *ad hominem* argument, contending that since the historian was not himself religious, she wanted to find skepticism in a distant time as well. This fallacy, of course, is based on attacking the person making the argument rather than on the logic or evidence supporting it. Avoid the temptation. Be fair to opposing views, describe them accurately, and criticize them on their merits.

And you should also eschew the bandwagon fallacy, the easy assumption that because many historians agree on an issue, they must be right. Consensus by experts is not to be scorned. But experts can also be prone to prejudices or succumb to a desire not to be alone in their opinions. The democratic desire to seek a majority opinion is not always the best way to arrive at historical conclusions. Great historical work has been done by people who went doggedly in pursuit of evidence against the influence of a historical consensus. But be sure you have the evidence when you attack a consensus!

MAKING INFERENCES

We certainly want to encourage you to apply your mind to your evidence and also, in questioning your sources, to utilize the ability of the mind to infer. Humans manage their daily lives by making inferences. If in the morning you see low, dark clouds piled in the sky, when you leave home, you take along an umbrella. Why? You have seen such clouds before, and they have often meant rain. You infer by calling on past experience to interpret a present event or situation. You cannot always be certain that what you infer is true. Sometimes black clouds blow away quickly, leaving the skies clear so that you lug around a useless umbrella and maybe a raincoat all day long. But without inference humans would have to reinvent the world every morning.

Historians always infer some answers to their questions. They strive to make sense of a document, of other evidence, or of inconsistencies between several sources. They try to decide exactly what is reliable and to understand why the evidence was created, when it might have been, where, and by whom. The aim of inference is coherence. Historians try to fit what they know into a plausible whole. For example, you would likely infer that there is something fishy about documents that use words not coined until long after the purported age of the document itself. Suppose you read this sentence in the diary of a pioneer woman who supposedly crossed the plains on her way to California in 1851: "We are having a very hard time, and I know that Americans who drive through Nebraska in years to come on Interstate 80 will scarcely imagine what we have endured." You would immediately infer that something is seriously wrong with the claims of this document!

In practice, historians face similar problems in dealing with all sorts of evidence. This is particularly true when the written documents are missing, are not very helpful, or seem to be inconsistent. But that does not keep a good historian from asking questions, and making inferences, in trying to tell a true story about the past. For example, after reading accounts of Hernando de Soto's sixteenth-century journey through what is now the southeastern United States, Alfred W. Crosby was struck by the inconsistencies between those descriptions and the accounts of the first intended settlers two centuries later:

> In eastern and southern Arkansas and northeastern Louisiana, where De Soto found thirty towns and provinces, the French found only a handful of villages. Where De Soto had been able to stand on one temple mound and see several villages with their mounds and little else but fields of maize between, there was now wilderness. . . .
>
> In the sixteenth century, De Soto's chroniclers saw no buffalo along their route from Florida to Tennessee and back to the coast, or if they did see those wonderful beasts, they did not mention them—which

seems highly improbable. Archeological evidence and examination of Amerindian place names also indicate there were no buffalo along the De Soto route, nor between it and salt water. A century and a half later, when the French and English arrived, they found the shaggy animals in at least scattered herds from the mountains to the Gulf and even to the Atlantic. What had happened in the interim is easy to explain in the abstract: An econiche opened up, and the buffalo moved into it. Something had kept these animals out of the expanse of parklike clearings in the forest that periodic Amerindian use of fire and hoe had created. That something had declined or disappeared after 1540. That something was, in all likelihood, the Amerindians themselves, who naturally would have killed the buffalo for food and to protect their crops.

The cause of that decline and disappearance was probably epidemic disease. No other factor seems capable of having exterminated so many people over such a large part of North America.[2]

Crosby's questions led him to seek additional information—in this case from ecology and geography—and then arrive at an answer on the basis of probable inference. Similar examples of inference abound in the writing of history on any subject.

Quantitative Data and History

Even some sources that on their surface seem to offer uncontroverted certainty often require the historian to reach conclusions by inference. This is certainly true in use of statistics, which in recent years have become a major source for writing history. Modern governments keep statistics with nearly religious passion, and other agencies, such as various polling organizations, collect statistics with the same avid compulsion. To some students of history, statistics seem tedious; to others they are exciting and open new windows to the past. But statistics require interpretation. "Like all data,"

---

2 Alfred W. Crosby, *Ecological Imperialism: The Biological Expansion of Europe, 900–1900* (Cambridge: Cambridge University Press, 1986), 212–213. We have omitted Crosby's citation of his considerable evidence.

warns Priya Joshi, a historian of British India, "statistics ought to be regarded as approximations at best, only as good as the tools to retrieve and manipulate them, and therefore only provisional until different or better statistics—or different or better methods of historical inquiry—emerge."[3] What historians infer from statistical data may reveal a great deal, but if historians infer badly, they can make serious errors.

One of the more controversial historical studies based on statistics in recent years was *Time on the Cross: The Economics of American Negro Slavery* by Robert Fogel and Stanley Engerman, an effort to see the face of slavery by looking at statistics from slave days before the Civil War. This method, known since the mid-twentieth century as "cliometrics"—the study of human history primarily from the analysis of statistical, and especially economic, data—was given extraordinary prominence after the publication of *Time on the Cross*.[4] In writing about *Truth in History*, Professor Oscar Handlin discussed the contention of Fogel and Engerman that the average age of slave mothers when they gave birth to their first child was 22.5 years. Handlin pointed out that Fogel and Engerman drew their data from wills probated in "fifty-four counties in eight Southern States between 1775 and 1865 which enumerated 80,000 slaves."[5]

Eighty thousand is a considerable figure. One might assume that statistical data drawn from such a sampling would have validity. But what about the significance the authors put on their finding that the average age of slave mothers was 22.5 years? They argued that slave mothers were mature women at the birth of their first child

[3] Priya Joshi, "Quantitative Method, Literary History," *Book History*, 5 (2002): 273.

[4] Robert William Fogel and Stanley L. Engerman, *Time on the Cross: The Economics of American Negro Slavery*, 2 vols. (Boston: Little, Brown, 1974). The authors describe Volume 1 as "the primary volume" of their work, containing a general discussion of the issues and their conclusions; Volume 2 was reserved for evidence and detailed "technological, methodological, and theoretical bases" of the study; vol. 1, p. v.

[5] Oscar Handlin, *Truth in History* (Cambridge, MA: Harvard University Press, 1981), 211.

and, therefore, they must have been married. This fairly late age for the first birth would indicate a stable family life. Yet that is not clear, although Fogel and Engerman use this evidence to infer that sexual promiscuity among slaves was limited and that family life was close and enduring. Handlin argues that such an elaborate conclusion cannot be drawn from the evidence.[6]

More recently, other historians have refined the use of statistical data. In her book on a similar subject, *Life in Black and White: Family and Community in the Slave South,* Professor Brenda E. Stevenson studied black and white families in Loudon County, Virginia, before the Civil War when tobacco plantations formed the basis of the economy. Using court records and business ledgers, including those in which records of white plantation owners were kept, she analyzed the effects of gender on the antebellum slave economy. At first black males predominated, but later black women began to be brought in, allowing slave families to develop. But then the white owners, strapped for cash as Virginia lost its markets for tobacco, began selling off children of slaves to the booming cotton economy of the deep South. Her statistics provide yet another window into the nature of a slave system where, as Stevenson concludes, "Virginia slave families, after all, essentially were not nuclear and did not derive from long-term monogamous marriages."[7]

As these two studies make clear, the near worship of statistics by modern bureaucratic societies makes the task of historians both easier and harder today. The task is easier because statistical information is now often available in precise, accessible, and usable forms, although sometimes the quantity of statistical information available may seem daunting. Anyone may feel overwhelmed by a

---

[6] Handlin, pp. 210–226. Although Handlin does acknowledge that "after publication Fogel and Engerman qualified the conclusion" (p. 210), this is only part of the lengthy criticism he directs against the use of statistical data in *Time on the Cross.*

[7] Brenda E. Stevenson, *Life in Black and White: Family and Community in the Slave South* (New York: Oxford University Press, 1996), 325.

project that can involve seemingly endless tables of numbers, charts, and graphs. The interpretation of such statistical data requires a high level of skill, and this can make the task even harder than it seems at first. Statistics as a discipline is substantial and complex, involving a rigorous introduction to the methods of interpreting statistics to make sense. Even with such instruction, errors in interpretation are not uncommon. Numbers may provide a comforting appearance of exactitude, but the appearance may not match the reality.

Some questions are beyond the power of statistics to measure. Many critics of quantitative methods in writing history protest that its practitioners claim to know more about the past than they really do. Nothing takes the place, say the critics, of understanding history through the lively words of those who participated in it. To these more humanistically inclined historians, statistics are skeletons without muscle and breath. Quantitative historians reply that the humanistic historians often argue about the same old things and that if statistics are often inexact, they often "tell a truth that would not otherwise be evident."[8] No doubt statistics can help unlock some historical puzzles. Thus our advice is the same as that offered more than three decades ago by David Hackett Fischer: "every historian should count everything he can, by the best available statistical method."[9]

Doing so requires that you understand the limits of statistical analysis and operate within those limits. If you write an essay based on quantitative research, be sure that you have enough data and that you know enough about interpreting statistics to avoid obvious errors. Learn the correct terminology for statistical analysis. (You must know the difference between the median and the average, the significance of the bell curve, and how a random sample is collected.) And be cautious in the inferences you draw from your evidence. Even if you have some knowledge of basic statistics,

---

[8] Joshi, 264.
[9] Fischer, 90.

be sure you understand how such methods are used in historical writing.[10] And do not be afraid to ask an expert. You probably have several faculty members at your university or college who teach statistics in one form or another and who understand the pitfalls of statistical research. Go talk to one of them about your essay. He or she will probably be delighted with your interest.

When using statistical data—or any other evidence—to make an inference important to your study of the sources, you become an active questioner. You don't read, or analyze, your sources passively. You read them actively, trying to fill in the gaps you always find in them and making inferences as you do so. In the process, you should also be assessing their value in helping to tell the story about the past that you want to write.

EVALUATING MATERIALS

Such an evaluation process is, of course, essential to historical writing. All historians, in one way or another, engage in making assessments of the materials they use in crafting their histories. These practices constitute the "critical method" of history, a key part of historians' special way of thinking. For many years they separated this critical method into two parts, frequently called "external criticism" and "internal criticism." Taken together they constitute nothing so much as a healthy historical skepticism in evaluating historical sources.

External criticism was originally an effort to determine if historical documents were, in fact, genuine, that they were what they purported to be. At one time this was extremely important, as in the case of a medieval document known as the Donation of Constantine. According to the document, the Emperor Constantine

---

10 As a starting point, we recommend Charles H. Feinstein and Mark Thomas, *Making History Count: A Primer in Quantitative Methods for Historians* (New York: Cambridge University Press, 2002).

was cured of leprosy by a pope, and in gratitude moved from Rome to Constantinople, writing out this document which gave political control of western Europe to the pope and his successors. The document was cited to prove the superiority of popes over kings in Europe for many years.

In the fifteenth century, an Italian named Lorenzo Valla began to ask some questions about the Donation. Why did none of the people around Constantine who wrote about him and his reign mention his attack of leprosy or the Donation? Why did the document use words that were not coined until centuries later? Why was it not quoted by anyone until about the ninth century? Why did it make many historical errors? Valla inferred the work could not be about an actual historical event and that it could not have been written in the time of Constantine. Therefore he concluded that the work was a forgery, and his judgment has been widely accepted ever since.

But the record of counterfeit historical documents is not limited to those created centuries ago. There are a number of well-known and more recent examples of primary sources which were not what they seemed to be. One involves the fascinating story of Sir Edmund Backhouse, an eccentric English orientalist, described by historian Hugh Trevor-Roper as *The Hermit of Peking*. Backhouse had long been considered a leading scholar of early twentieth-century Chinese history. His reputation rested on his command of the Chinese language and the good fortune to have discovered a number of important documents that served as the basis of his writings. He was also a benefactor of the Bodleian Library at Oxford University, donating some of those manuscripts—and a large number of others—to its China collections. He also penned a long memoir, which almost thirty years after his death in 1944 also found its way to the Bodleian. But because his biographical reflections were considered by many who saw them to be—even by the quietly permissive English upper class standards of his own time—somewhat obscene, it fell to Trevor-Roper, Regis Professor of Modern History at Oxford, to analyze them. In doing so, he produced a sort of literary biography concluding that Backhouse was not an extraordinarily gifted figure—unless it was as a forger! Trevor-Roper exposed the key documents Backhouse used in his most well known works as the result of an elaborate hoax and the Chinese texts themselves as forgeries.

Trevor-Roper asked the obvious historian's question: Why would Backhouse perpetrate, and through his also invented memoir, try to perpetuate such a hoax? His conclusion about Backhouse's motives is revealing: "History was to him not a discipline, a means of understanding the world, but a compensation, a means of escape from it."[11] Not only does this suggest much about the man who did so; it also suggests something about why such a hoax might be attractive to other would-be historical pranksters. But in this case there is also an instructive sequel, one we believe offers an incentive for caution to any writer of history.

Six years after the appearance of his book on Backhouse, Professor Trevor-Roper was drawn into another case of a disputed historical document. In April 1983, the German magazine *Stern* published excerpts from the extensive, newly discovered diaries of Adolf Hitler. As you might imagine, this caused a sensation. Were these the genuine handiwork of the Fürher himself? Many important historians were asked for their evaluation of the diaries. Drawing on his considerable experience, Trevor-Roper offered this opinion on the Hitler diaries:

> Whereas signatures, single documents, or even groups of documents can be skillfully forged, a whole coherent archive covering 35 years is far less easily manufactured.
>
> Such a disproportionate and indeed extravagant effort offers too large and vulnerable a flank to the critics who will undoubtedly assail it. . . . The archive, in fact, is not only a collection of documents which can be individually tested: it coheres as a whole and the diaries are an integral part of it.
>
> That is the internal evidence of authenticity.[12]

---

11 Hugh Trevor-Roper, *The Hermit of Peking* (New York: Knopf, 1977), 294.

12 Quoted in Dave Gross, "The Hitler Diaries" (n.d.) Culture-Jammer's Encyclopedia, http://www.sniggle.net/kujau.php (accessed 13 April 2006).

But Professor Trevor-Roper, it transpired, was actually duped by yet another clever forgery! And he was not the only one taken in by the forger, who capitalized on the widespread fascination with Hitler and the Nazis to create not just the diaries but other phony Hitler memorabilia as well. While financial gain probably was the forger's major motivation, certainly he had a similar disrespect for history as a disciplined inquiry as did Edmund Backhouse. And at least for a time, the hoax convinced even as distinguished, and skeptical, a historian as Trevor-Roper.

While his experiences should suggest that you would be well-served by a healthy historical skepticism, it is unlikely you will have to make many such judgments about the authenticity of the primary sources that you use in writing your history papers. Perhaps if your sources were found in a discarded trunk or an abandoned attic, you will need to make an effort to determine if they are authentic. But many of the primary sources you are likely to employ will be found in published collections. You may reasonably expect the editors will have undertaken a careful external criticism of the documents prior to their publication. You may actually find other, unpublished primary sources in nearby archives or libraries, where the custodians of the original documents will have made such determinations. Lest these assurances give a false sense of security, remember you will still need to engage further in the historians' critical method, retaining the same sense of skepticism as you apply the historians' questions—*who, what, when, where,* and *why*—to all of your sources.

In doing so you can use those questions, along with the answers you find and the careful inferences you make, to help establish first if your sources are *plausible* and *trustworthy*, and then if they are *accurate* and can be *corroborated*. Those four standards of evaluation will serve you well as you read, and ask questions about, a wide variety of both secondary as well as primary sources, including those you find on the Internet and in other electronic media, where there are no librarians or archivists, and usually no editors who have made preliminary evaluations of materials. Instead, with all sources you find on the World Wide Web, *you* must assume the role of primary evaluator of the information you find. Your readers, and especially your instructors, will expect you to do so carefully.

Certainly the common sense test is one of the best you have at your disposal to begin your evaluations. Historians do have to trust their own insights. They need to make reasonable judgments based on their own sense of what is possible. Does your common sense tell you that what you have read is truly plausible? Could it really have happened as your sources would have it? If your sources suggest that the Egyptian pyramids or the great stone statues on Easter Island where created by alien visitors from outer space, you have good reason to doubt them. The more fantastic the explanations offered, the more likely they will be little more than simple fantasy. One application of this common sense rule is the philosophical and scientific principle known as *Ockham's razor,* after the ideas of the fourteenth-century English philosopher William of Ockham. Simply put, the concept suggests that simpler explanations are usually to be preferred over complex ones, especially when known information can be used to reach those simpler conclusions.

Yet even when you apply your mind in this way to determine if your source is plausible, what leads you to trust your sources? Were those doing the reporting in a position to know what they reported? For example, were American veterans of the Korean War who reported Korean civilians were indiscriminately shot by U.S. soldiers actually serving in military units present at No Gun Re, where other Korean civilians claimed the attacks took place? Did any of the soldiers have special knowledge of the situation that would lend credibility to their testimony? Perhaps some of them served as medical corpsmen and treated the wounded. That might make their statements more trustworthy in your eyes. And in the case of secondary accounts, do they come from authors whose works have generally been considered reliable? You may have to check reviews of some historical books to help determine this, although depending on any single review would likely not be the wisest course. The widespread availability of databases such as JSTOR and Project Muse make such efforts much easier, and you should use them in making evaluations of your sources.

You can also make your own determination by reading carefully to see if all the details fit together. Are the descriptions of times and places accurate? Do the details match what is known and what can reasonably be inferred? In many British colonial territories, annual census figures remained the same year after year with no variation. District colonial administrators, it seems, did little more than make estimates and repeat them when new figures were required a year later, disregarding the improbability that births and deaths would exactly balance year after year. While few supervising officials in the British Colonial Office questioned such reporting, no historian would today consider such statistics to be an accurate reflection of a region's actual population.

But for some other details it might be possible for you to seek corroborating evidence. Good historians generally try to do this, just as *Washington Post* reporters Bob Woodward and Carl Bernstein always sought other sources to confirm the details which their famous informant, Deep Throat, passed on to them concerning what has come to be known as the Watergate affair of the 1970s. For over thirty years the reporters did not disclose that top FBI official Mark Felt was their source; yet the great care they used in corroborating his information stood up to years of scrutiny, both before and after the revelation of Felt's identity in 2005. Keep in mind, though, your corroborating sources must be independent of each other if you wish to have real confidence in the accuracy of what you write. This does not mean that a single source must always be rejected. But without corroboration, you must establish through other applications of your critical methodology that your sources are accurate.

While it is true that good historians do not implicitly trust their sources, neither do they trust their own first impressions. Nor do they merely pose random questions regarding what they read, what they hear, or what they see. The exercise of the historian's critical method demands a much more systematic application of the injunctions to ask questions and make inferences. Only in doing so can you really claim to have evaluated your source materials and to have written an essay presenting a story about the past which makes any claim to being true. Nothing is quite so destructive to historians' reputations as presenting conclusions that do more to prove their own gullibility, laziness, or unwillingness to ask questions than to provide real insight into the meaning of the past. You can make a start at avoiding such appearances by keeping in mind the following checklist as you begin researching and thinking about sources for a new writing project:

Writer's Checklist

_____   ✔ Can I be certain this source is genuine?

_____   ✔ What questions do I need to ask about this source?

_____   ✔ Is the information truly *plausible*?

_____   ✔ Am I confident the source is *trustworthy*?

_____   ✔ Are the details in the source *accurate*?

_____   ✔ Do I have any *corroborating evidence*?

MODES OF HISTORICAL WRITING

■ ■ ■

Like other writers, historians use the four common modes of expression: (1) *description,* (2) *narration,* (3) *exposition,* and (4) *argument.* Of these, argument is nearly always the most important mode in college classes, but not to the exclusion of the others. In its most basic meaning, though, argument does not suggest a dispute about something. The word originally meant *to prove* or *to assert.* At an earlier time people spoke of the "argument" of a novel, meaning the novel's plot and the view of human nature and possibility that informed the writer's way of presenting the story. Even today, in written prose, argument is a principle of organization that unites facts and observations to present a proposition important to the writer. Instructors will expect you to have a *thesis,* a point of view, a main idea that unites your essay, a proposition you want others to believe. (*Thesis* comes from a Greek word meaning *to set down.*) Your thesis will be the argument, the reason you write the essay, the case you want to prove.

To make your argument convincing, you will need to present evidence supporting your point of view. But we should offer a fundamental caution. A mere collection of facts, specific pieces of information, is not an essay nor would it constitute an argument. The distinguished historian Barbara Tuchman was very clear about the temptations which "facts" offer to all historians:

> To offer a mass of undigested facts, of names not identified and places not located, is of no use to the reader and is simple laziness on the part

of the author, or pedantry to show how much he has read. To discard the unnecessary requires courage and also extra work. . . . The historian is continually being beguiled down fascinating byways and sidetracks. But the art of writing—the test of the artist—is to resist the beguilement and cleave to the subject.[1]

The facts cannot be an end in themselves. They must be carefully selected and woven together in such a way that they support a well-defined point of view that the writer wishes other people to believe. If you take notes on your reading and assemble a vast collection of historical facts about, say, Woodrow Wilson, you don't have an essay. But if you sift through your notes and discover that Wilson often expressed negative attitudes toward black Americans, you begin to have a thesis for an essay, something you want to examine more carefully. Why did Wilson have these attitudes? What did he do in response to them? What consequences did his attitudes and his actions have? It may be that hardly any scholars have considered this aspect of Wilson's career. So when you write your own essay on the subject, you may not be arguing with anyone else. That is, you may not have a disputation or a debate with another historian on the subject. Still, your point of view is an argument.

As you study the modes we describe below, keep in mind that argument, in the sense of developing a thesis, is fundamental to all the modes used in writing history essays. The modes overlap, and you may use all of them in a single essay; certainly we have in our own writing. A descriptive paragraph might give details of a marsh near Boston's Back Bay and the chill of an unusually cold New England spring in 1775. A narrative paragraph may tell how British troops ferried across the Back Bay on the night of April 18, 1775, were required to stand in the marsh with water up to their knees waiting for supplies they did not need before they tramped out to Lexington and Concord.

---

[1] Barbara Tuchman, "In Search of History," in *Practicing History* (New York: Ballantine Books, 1982), 18. This is actually the text of a 1963 address Tuchman gave at Radcliffe College.

A brief exposition might consider the effects on tempers of soldiers having to march 12 or 15 miles to Lexington in cold, wet clothes and heavy wet boots. A writer might then argue that the needless delay in the Cambridge marsh robbed the British of the element of surprise and led to their humiliating defeat at the hands of the American minutemen in the battles that began the Revolutionary War.

Although the four modes often overlap, they are distinct; one will usually predominate in a given essay or book. When you write an essay, try to determine which modes will best advance your argument. If you have a clear idea of the mode best suited to your purposes, you make the task easier for you and your readers.

DESCRIPTION

Description presents an account of sensory experience—the way things look, feel, taste, sound, and smell—as well as more impressionistic descriptions of attitudes and behavior. Popular history includes vivid descriptions, and you can describe people and places with great effect in an essay intended for a college or scholarly audience. No matter how learned or unlearned in the limitless facts of a historical period, everyone has had sensory experiences similar to those of people in the past. Senses are the common denominator in human life. Perhaps as a consequence of reliance on sense experience and observations, readers like concrete details about physical reality in books and articles about history. Details reassure your readers that the world of the past was enough like their own world to imagine it, to place themselves within it (for at least a moment), and to find it familiar and understandable.

Description is useful to kindle the imagination of readers and draw them into the story you wish to tell. Jonathan Spence does exactly that as he begins his study of life in seventeenth-century provincial China, *The Death of Woman Wang*:

> The earthquake struck T'an-ch'eng on July 25, 1668. It was evening, the moon just rising. There was no warning, save for a frightening roar that

seemed to come from somewhere to the northwest. The buildings in the city began to shake and the trees took up a rhythmical swaying, tossing ever more wildly back and forth until their tips almost touched the ground. Then came one sharp violent jolt that brought down stretches of the city walls and battlements, officials' yamens [or residences], temples, and thousands of private homes. Broad fissures opened up across the streets and underneath the houses. Jets of water spurted into the air to a height of twenty feet or more, and streams of water poured down the roads and flooded the irrigation ditches. Those who tried to remain standing felt as if their feet were round stones spinning out of control and were brought crashing to the ground. . . .

As suddenly as it had come the earthquake departed. The ground was still. The water seeped away, leaving the open fissures edged with mud and fine sand. The ruins rested in layers where they had fallen, like giant sets of steps.[2]

All these descriptions of the earthquake will resonate with any reader who has likewise lived through such an experience and also with those who understand earthquakes only from seeing images of them and their aftermath on television. The vivid descriptions will make it easy for you to imagine that you are transported to eastern China more than three centuries ago. And by introducing his study with such clear and believable descriptions, Professor Spence has prepared you to trust his analysis of life in a society that is likely far different from any of your experiences. You can often accomplish much the same effect in your essays by careful attention to description.

But never make things up when you describe something. Although some readers may be entertained by flights of fancy in historical writing, historians find them cheap and dishonest, and with good reason. Here are two paragraphs written by the late Paul Murray Kendall in his laudatory biography of Richard III, king of England between 1483 and 1485. They describe actions and emotions during the battle of Barnet on the morning of April 14, 1471,

---

2 Jonathan D. Spence, *The Death of Woman Wang* (New York: Viking Press: 1978), 1–2.

in which Richard, then Duke of Gloucester, fought on the side of his older brother, Edward IV, against an effort by the Earl of Warwick to overthrow King Edward.

> Suddenly there was a swirl in the mist to the left of and behind the enemy position. A shiver ran down the Lancastrian line. Exeter's men began to give way, stubbornly at first, then faster. Warwick's center must be crumbling. Richard signaled his trumpeters. The call to advance banners rang out. The weary young commander and his weary men surged forward. Then the enemy were in full flight, casting away their weapons as they ran.
>
> Out of the mist loomed the great sun banner of the House of York. A giant figure strode forward. Pushing his visor up, Richard saw that the King was smiling at him in brotherly pride. The right wing, driving westward across the Lancastrian rear, had linked up with Edward's center to bring the battle to an end. It was seven o'clock in the morning; the struggle had lasted almost three hours.[3]

Kendall's description evokes a vivid image of battle, but his scene is almost entirely made up. The sources for the battle of Barnet are skimpy. It is agreed a mist lay over the ground and that the battle was confused. In the midst of the battle, someone on the Lancastrian side shouted "treason," and others took up the cry. The Lancastrian troops in the middle of the line, thinking one of their leaders on a flank had gone over to the enemy, broke and ran. Their commander, the Earl of Warwick, was killed while trying to catch his horse. But Kendall's description of Richard meeting his brother Edward is all fantasy. No wonder historian Charles Ross, in remarking on Kendall's account of Barnet, comments dryly, "The incautious reader might be forgiven for thinking that the author himself was present at the battle."[4]

Much worse than Ross's scorn is what such fictional details have done to Kendall's credibility. His book aims at resurrecting the reputation

---

[3] Paul Murray Kendall, *Richard the Third* (New York: Doubleday, 1965), 97.

[4] Charles Ross, *Richard III* (Berkeley and Los Angeles: University of California Press, 1983), 21.

of Richard III from Thomas More and Shakespeare who made him a lying hypocrite and a murderer, guilty of ordering the deaths of the little sons of Edward IV after the King died. To believe such an argument against a predominant historical opinion, you must have confidence in the author. But a book so filled with fictional descriptive detail as Kendall's cannot be taken seriously by dispassionate and thoughtful readers, and it has been regularly ridiculed since its publication.

It is also important not to allow your descriptions to fall into familiar and accepted patterns of thought in an attempt to invoke what you think your reader might expect. Such an approach also runs the risk of undermining your credibility. Rather, you should tailor your descriptions to paint the mental pictures you intend to be true, based on the best evidence available to you. In the following paragraphs Professor Ken Wolf does this explicitly in describing the army—frequently referred to in much historical literature as a "horde"—of Genghis Khan, the great Mongol leader.

> Our word *horde*, taken from the Mongol *ordu*, meaning camp or field army, suggests a huge body of dirty, undisciplined barbarians, drinking mare's blood, shooting on the run, and defeating their enemies by sheer weight of numbers. Such was not the case. Mongol armies under Genghis Khan *never* outnumbered those of their enemies; they were successful due to "splendid organization, discipline, leadership, and morale." We should add skill, for the Mongols were probably the most skilled horse soldiers of the pre-industrial age. They learned to ride their famous ponies at age three, and they began using a bow and arrow at age four or five. The adult Mongol cavalryman could shoot an arrow with deadly accuracy over a hundred yards; he could do this riding full gallop and even, when necessary, retreating and shooting over his shoulder; a high saddle and stirrups (a Mongol invention later adopted in the West) kept him from falling. Mongol armies could ride for days without stopping to cook food. They carried kumis, dried milk curd, cured meant, and water and could eat, drink, and sleep on horseback. . . .
>
> Genghis Khan used a decimal organization. Divisions, or *toumen*, of ten thousand men were divided into regiments of one thousand; these were then subdivided into squads of 100 and patrols, or *arban*, of ten men each. Each unit commander gave strict obedience to his superior,

on pain of death. In campaigns, *toumens* could travel in widely separated columns and unite quickly in battle.[5]

Wolf begins with familiar images, usually conjuring up unpleasant thoughts of little more than groups of wild men. But then he sets about calling those stereotypes into question. He continues with a much more straightforward description of Mongol soldiers, attempting to replace unfortunate images he believes readers may hold with others which he is confident represent something closer to reality. In doing so he is careful to avoid any explicitly evocative language, appealing instead to simple images you might well recognize from your own experiences. And when you finish reading his description of the Mongol cavalrymen you likely will better understand the argument that is the foundation of his essay.

When you write descriptive passages in your essays, always consider the questions below.

Writer's Checklist

_____ ✔ Do my descriptions reflect sensory experience?
_____ ✔ Do they bring ordinary, or at least widespread, memories to mind?
_____ ✔ Are the impressions and emotions I evoke common enough to be recognizable?
_____ ✔ Have I based my descriptions on sound evidence?
_____ ✔ Have I avoided stereotypical descriptions in favor of more accurate ones?

NARRATIVE

As important as both making a point and providing clear descriptions are, narratives tell stories, and stories are the bedrock of history. Without narratives, history would die as a discipline. Narratives tell

---

[5] Ken Wolf, "Genghis Khan: Incomparable Nomad Conqueror," in *Personalities and Problems: Interpretive Essays in World Civilizations,* 2d ed. (Boston: McGraw Hill College, 1999), 1:91–92; we have omitted Wolf's footnotes.

us what happened, usually following the sequence of events as they happen, one event after the other—just as you tell a story about something that happened to you this morning.

Good narrative history often looks easy to write because it is easy to read. In fact, storytelling is a complicated art. As in description, part of the art lies in a sense of what to include and what to exclude, what to believe and what to reject. Narrative must also take into account contradictions in the evidence and either resolve them or admit frankly that they cannot be resolved. Who fired the first shot on the morning of April 19, 1775, when British regular soldiers clashed with the minutemen on the Lexington Green in Massachusetts? The incident makes a nice subject for narrative history—but it is not an easy story to write. Sylvanus Wood, one of the minutemen, dictated his account of the battle over fifty years after he fought in it under the command of Captain John Parker. Here is part of what he said:

> Parker led those of us who were equipped to the north end of Lexington Common, near the Bedford Road, and formed us in single file. I was sta-tioned about in the centre of the company. While we were standing, I left my place and went from one end of the company to the other and counted every man who was paraded, and the whole number was thirty-eight and no more. . . .
>
> The British troops approached us rapidly in platoons with a gen-eral officer on horseback at their head. The officer came up to within about two rods [a little more than thirty feet] of the centre of the com-pany, where I stood, the first platoon being about three rods distant. They were halted. The officer then swung his sword, and said, "Lay down your arms, you damned rebels, or you are all dead men. Fire!" Some guns were fired by the British at us from the first platoon, but no person was killed or hurt, being probably charged only with powder.
>
> Just at this time, Captain Parker ordered every man to take care of himself. The company immediately dispersed; and while the company was dispersing and leaping over the wall, the second platoon of the British fired and killed some of our men. There was not a gun fired by any of Captain Parker's company, within my knowledge.[6]

---

6 Quoted in *The Spirit of Seventy-Six*, eds. Henry Steele Commager and Richard B. Morris (New York: Harper and Row, 1975), 82–83.

Paul Revere had been captured by the British in the middle of the night before the skirmish. He told the British that 500 men would be waiting for them in Lexington. Lieutenant John Barker of the British Army was with the British regiment called the King's Own. He wrote an account of the battle only a few days afterward, and here is part of what he said:

> About 5 miles on this side of a town called Lexington, which lay in our road, we heard there were some hundreds of people collected together intending to oppose us and stop our going on. At 5 o'clock we arrived there and saw a number of people, I believe between 2 and 300, formed in a common in the middle of the town. We still continued advancing, keeping prepared against an attack tho' without intending to attack them; but on our coming near them they fired one or two shots, upon which our men without any orders rushed in upon them, fired and put 'em to flight. Several of them were killed, we could not tell how many because they were got behind walls and into the woods. We had a man of the 10th Light Infantry wounded, nobody else hurt.[7]

How many American minutemen waited for the British on the green at Lexington that morning? The writer of a historical narrative must deal with the contradiction. You cannot pretend that the contradiction does not exist. Professor David Hackett Fischer, who has written an excellent book on the battles, did what you should do when you face such a contradiction. He looked for more sources, and he discovered a number of other depositions given by members of the Lexington militia and eyewitnesses. These investigations allowed him to make a sensible inference: Many of the men the British soldiers saw as they advanced on Lexington were spectators, and some other minutemen joined Parker and his band after Sylvanus Wood counted the group. Here is part of Fischer's absorbing narrative. We have left out his numerous footnotes; however, note his careful citation of his sources in the text:

> At the same moment the British officers were studying the militia on the Common in front of them. Paul Revere's warning of 500 men in arms

---

[7] Quoted in *The Spirit of Seventy-Six*, 70–71.

echoed in their ears. As the officers peered through the dim gray light, the spectators to the right and left appeared to be militia too. Captain Parker's small handful of men multiplied in British eyes to hundreds of provincial soldiers. Pitcairn thought that he faced "near 200 of the rebels." Barker reckoned the number at "between two and three hundred."

On the other side, the New England men also inflated the size of the Regular force, which was magnified by the length of its marching formation on the narrow road. As the militia studied the long files of red-coated soldiers, some reckoned the force at between 1200 and 1500 men. In fact there were only about 238 of all ranks in Pitcairn's six companies, plus the mounted men of Mitchell's patrol, and a few supernumeraries.

The Lexington militia began to consult earnestly among themselves. Sylvanus Wood, a Woburn man who joined them, had made a quick count a few minutes earlier and found to his surprise that there were only thirty-eight militia in all. Others were falling into line, but altogether no more than sixty or seventy militia mustered on the Common, perhaps less. One turned to his captain and said, "There are so few of us it is folly to stand here."[8]

Fischer continues his absorbing story, working along the way to resolve the contradictions in his sources. By the time his readers get this far they have some understanding of why the British overestimated the patriot force. In a detailed appendix, Fischer explains why he rejects Barker's number of "about 600" men in the British attacking force: Fischer went to the payroll rosters of the British army to see how many soldiers of the King's Own were collecting wages for their service. He recognized, as all historians must, that developing a narrative can be a complicated task.

A good narrative begins by establishing some sort of tension, some kind of problem, that later development of the narrative should resolve. The beginning arouses readers' curiosity. It introduces elements in tension and the rest of the story dwells on resolving or explaining that tension. Do not introduce material into your essay at the beginning if you don't intend to do something with it

---

8 David Hackett Fischer, *Paul Revere's Ride* (New York and Oxford: Oxford University Press, 1994), 188–189.

later on. A narrative should also have a climax that embodies the meaning the writer wants readers to take from the story. At the climax, everything comes together, and the problem is solved or else explained. Because it gathers up all the threads and joins them to make the writer's point, the climax comes near the end of the essay, and your readers should feel that you have kept a promise made to them in the beginning. If you cannot find a climactic point in your narrative, you need to reorganize your story.

The story should move along, unburdened by unnecessary details. A good story can be enlivened by apt quotation, as in Fischer's narrative of the Battle of Lexington. But a principle of style worth remembering is that long block quotations frequently slow down a narrative, as does the inclusion of too many details. In telling a story, it is usually better to keep quotations short and pointed, and the examples limited, so that they clearly illustrate the events being recounted and readily lead to the conclusion you intend.

In the following narrative concerning the Battle of Adwa, fought in 1896 between Ethiopian forces of Emperor Menilek and Italian armies threatening to bring his country within Italy's northeastern African colonial orbit, Harold G. Marcus is spare in mentioning details and even more parsimonious in his use of quotation. He begins by indicating the plans of the Italian commander, General Oreste Baratieri, establishing an expectation of the outcome. Then he narrates the story of how the battle actually unfolded.

> The general and his army of 8,463 Italians and 10,749 Eriterans [local Africans] held the high ground between Adigrat and Idaga Hamus. Baratieri was prepared to outwit his enemy, whose limited supplies would have forced retirement southward, permitting Baratieri to claim victory and also advance deeper into Tigray. . . .
>   At 9:00 P.M., on 28 February, the Italians began a forced march to the three hills that dominated the Ethiopian camp, to surprise and challenge Menilek's army. To secure his left Baratieri sent his reserve brigade to an unnamed, nearby fourth hill, but the Ethiopian guide, either through misdirection or sabotage, led the Italians astray. Not only was the left flank uncovered but also a quarter of the Italian force was rendered useless and vulnerable. So, even if Baratieri's army had occupied

the high points and deployed in strong defensive positions on the frontal slopes, it was foredoomed to defeat. Indeed, the timing of the Italian attack, as a surprise on early Sunday morning, was all wrong.

At 4:00 A.M., on 1 March, Menilek, [Empress] Taitou, and the rases [chief political and military subordinates of the Emperor] were at mass, which the Orthodox church celebrates early. It was a sad time, since the food situation had forced the emperor to order camp to be struck on 2 March. His relief must have been great when a number of couriers and runners rushed in to report the enemy was approaching in force. The emperor ordered men to arms, and, as the soldiers lined up, priests passed before them hearing confession, granting absolution, and offering blessings. The green, orange, and red flags of Ethiopia were unfurled when the emperor appeared, and the soldiers cheered and cheered. At 5:30 A.M., Menilek's 100,000-man army moved forward, to confront an Italian force of 14,500 soldiers.

By 9:00 A.M., the outcome was obvious. The Italian center had crumbled, and other units were in danger of being flanked by Ethiopians who had found the gap in Baratieri's defenses. By noon, when retreat sounded, the Italians had paid dearly. Four thousand Europeans and 2,000 Eritreans had died, 1,428 of Baratieri's soldiers had been wounded, and 1,800 prisoners were held by the Ethiopians. All told, the Italian army lost 70 percent of its forces, a disaster for a modern army.

In sharp contrast, Menilek's forces suffered an estimated 4,000–7,000 killed and perhaps as many as 10,000 wounded, which made for an acceptably low loss ratio. The Italian enemy had been destroyed, whereas the Ethiopian army remained in being, strengthened by the weapons and matériel abandoned on the field. The victory was unequivocally Ethiopian.

In telling the story of this imperial encounter, Marcus poses a problem and then narrates the story to its unexpected conclusion. Although there are many other sources available concerning the conflict at Adwa, including Italian official records, letters and diaries of soldiers, not to mention oral testimonies collected from some of the participants, Marcus wisely elects not to infuse his narrative with too much of this potentially extraneous information. He uses just enough evidence—primarily the numbers of soldiers engaged in the battle and the numbers of casualties—in a way that lends credibility to his account. And thus you are disposed to believe him when he later goes on to conclude that Menilek's victory at the Battle of Adwa did "guarantee Ethiopia another generation and one-half of virtually unchallenged independence; it gave the country a status similar to that of Afghanistan, Persia, Japan, and Thailand as accepted anomalies in the imperialist world order."[9] And you can see how his battle narrative supports the essential argument he makes in his book.

Of course, in your research you might just as well consult some of the numerous published (and perhaps, if your college or university has its own archive, also unpublished) collections of letters, as well as journals and collected papers. They offer similar opportunities for narrative writing about other stories concerning the past. Not just battles, but also the lives of individuals, and even the explanations they offer for the circumstances of their existence, can become fascinating subjects for your history essays. Whatever sources you use, be sure to pose the questions below to yourself when you write historical narrative.

Writer's Checklist

_____ ✔ Why am I telling this story?
_____ ✔ What happened, why, and when did it begin and end?
_____ ✔ Who were the major characters in the drama?
_____ ✔ What details must I tell, and what can I leave out?
_____ ✔ What is the climax of the story?
_____ ✔ What does the story mean?

EXPOSITION

Expositions explain and analyze—philosophical ideas, the causes of events, the significance of decisions, the motives of participants, the working of an organization, the ideology of a political party. Any time you set out to explain cause and effect, or the meaning of an event or an idea, you write in the expository mode. Of course, exposition

---

9 Harold G. Marcus, *A History of Ethiopia,* updated ed. (Berkeley: University of California Press, 2002), 98–100.

may coexist in an essay with other modes. The narrator who tells *what* happened usually devotes some paragraphs to telling *why* it happened—and so goes into expository writing. Some historical essays are fairly evenly balanced between narrative and exposition, telling both what happened and why, explaining the significance of the story. Many historical essays are primarily expositions, especially those that break down and analyze a text or event to tell readers what it means—even as the author narrates what happened that makes the explanation necessary.

Often acknowledged as an outstanding example of historical writing, Garrett Mattingly's *The Armada*, includes a remarkable exposition on "The Ominous Year" when the Spanish King Philip II sent his famous Armada against the English crown:

> As the Year 1587 drew to a close, a shudder of apprehension ran across western Europe. In part it was a perfectly rational apprehension. . . .
>
> It had been discerned over a century before, perhaps many centuries before, and as 1588 approached, the awful rumor of impending disaster spread throughout western Europe. Basically the prophecy of doom depended on the numerology of the Revelation of John, clarified (if that is the right word) by hints in Daniel xii, and reinforced by a bloodcurdling passage in Isaiah. To those who had sufficiently studied the question there seemed to be no doubt that all history since the first year of Our Lord was divided into a series of cycles, complicated permutations of multiples of ten, and seven, each cycle terminated by some gigantic event, and the whole series closing with awful finality in 1588. . . .
>
> Spread from one end of Europe to the other, the prophecies about 1588 were differently received and differently interpreted according the country.[10]

In his full essay on the omens concerning the year 1588, Professor Mattingly draws together many strands of evidence from both religious and secular thought to analyze the mood in the capitals of Europe, making many inferences while also leaving open many

---

[10] Garrett Mattingly, *The Armada* (Boston: Houghton Mifflin, 1959), 172, 175, 177.

unanswered questions. That is as it should be in a skillful exposition, and there are many other examples in historical writing. Look for them, especially in the textbooks you are assigned to read for your courses.

In college essays about history, exposition usually plays an important role. You may, for example, write to answer this question: What did the founding fathers mean by the Second Amendment to the U.S. Constitution? That amendment reads, "A well-regulated militia being necessary to the security of a free State, the right of the people to keep and bear arms shall not be infringed." The essay you write in response would be an exposition. But it would probably include some narratives, perhaps the situation in 1789 when the Constitution was ratified, the situation today, or the decisions of courts in the past on cases brought under the Second Amendment.

There are many other possibilities that you might choose. The study of the influence of one thinker on another ("A comparison between Thomas More's *Utopia* and Nicolo Machiavelli's *The Prince*"), or of one set of ideas on a historical process ("The view of human nature expressed in the *Federalist Papers*"), can make a good expository essay. You may even analyze the significance of some technological invention ("The Role of Steamboats in the European Colonization of Africa"). All these subjects require analysis of texts, of events, or both. To write a good history essay on any of these topics you must explain things, relate various texts to one another, make inferences, and perhaps ask some questions that no one can answer. But that difficulty does not stop the historian from trying to answer the questions.

One important category of expository writing, especially in college courses, is the historiographic essay. These "histories of histories," as they are sometimes called, can be very important in helping students understand the evidence and arguments historians have used when considering a particular topic or some corollary of it. Students are often asked to write such essays, though we have found that many of our students frequently find such an exercise very difficult. Perhaps this is because they prefer to stick to the facts, and treating ideas themselves as facts in such an essay sometimes seems overwhelming. But you should not be fearful of such an effort. If you approach it as simply another form of historical analysis, it won't be as difficult as you may at first imagine.

There are many examples of historiographic essays in a wide variety of historical journals; you would do well to look for them and familiarize yourself with this common form of historical writing. Many contain detailed analyses which cannot be usefully illustrated in a short excerpt, but this selection from a recent essay by David Brion Davis will give you some idea of how to approach a historiographic expositions:

> During the past thirty years, our understanding of American slavery has been extraordinarily enriched by numerous studies that fall in the . . . category of rigorous and sustained comparison. One thinks particularly of the work of Carl Degler comparing slavery and race relations in Brazil and the United States; George M. Fredrickson's two volumes on white supremacy and its consequences in the United States and South Africa; and Peter Kolchin's comparison and analysis of American slavery and Russian serfdom, a project that greatly broadened and enriched his subsequent survey of American slavery from 1619 to 1877. Mention should also be made of more specialized studies, such as those by Shearer Davis Bowman on U.S. planters and Prussian Junkers, by Eugene D. Genovese and Michael Craton on slave rebellions, and by Richard S. Dunn on two specific plantations in Virginia and Jamaica. While the comparative method *can* lead to mechanical listings of similarities and differences, it would clearly be useful to have more comparative studies on such specific subjects as domestic servants, slave artisans, and slaves in urban and manufacturing jobs. Peter Kolchin has candidly pointed to the severe problems comparative history faces, problems that help to explain the somewhat limited number of such full-length studies; yet I think that the cumulative benefit of comparative work can be seen in the global awareness of historians such as Thomas Holt, when writing on Jamaica; Rebecca Scott, when writing on Brazil and Cuba; Frederick Cooper, when writing on East Africa; and Seymour Drescher, when writing on British abolitionism and other subjects—to say nothing of the omnipresent economic historian Stanley L. Engerman, whose work on various forms of unfree labor could hardly be broader in perspective.

But while careful, empirical comparison is indispensable, especially in alerting us to the importance of such matters as the demography and sex ratios of slave societies, the differences in slave communities, and the social implications of resident as opposed to absentee planters, much recent research has also underscored the importance of "the Big Picture"—the interrelationships that constituted an Atlantic Slave System as well as the place of such racial slavery in the evolution of the Western and modern worlds.[11]

Of course, Davis brings the experience of a distinguished career in writing about slavery to his historiographic exposition. Yet the works he mentions would be easily accessible to a student searching for histories written on the subject of slavery, and the categories he uses to group the studies would be readily observable to anyone who read them carefully. Professor Davis continues with consideration of numerous other works on the subject of his essay, "Slavery from Broader Perspectives," but he might just as well have analyzed and compared the arguments in the twenty books and articles he mentions. The latter effort would, as well, have resulted in a thoughtful historiographic essay, and one within the scope of many undergraduates of our acquaintance. By applying your mind to careful research and thoughtful reading you could also create a similarly substantial exposition about how historians have, over time, written about slavery—or almost any other serious subject.

When you decide to write an exposition on a particular subject in one of your essays, be sure to reflect on these questions:

Writer's Checklist

_____ ✔ Why is this explanation necessary?
_____ ✔ Have I provided a context for this analysis?

---

11 David Brion Davis, "*AHR Forum:* Looking at Slavery from Broader Perspectives," *The American Historical Review* 105 (2000): 453–454; we have omitted Professor Davis's footnotes, which include complete citations to the many works he mentions.

_____   ✔ Have I clearly identified the crucial causes and/or
significance?

_____   ✔ Are my inferences credible and plausible?

_____   ✔ Have I clarified essential terms and the meaning
of what I am explaining?

ARGUMENT

Historians and others use argument in their writing to take a position on a controversial subject. As we suggested at the start of this chapter, it can be said that every essay contains an argument since every essay is built around a proposition that the writer wants us to believe. Yet in common usage, an argument is part of a debate, a dialogue between opposing views—sometimes many opposing views. Arguments include exposition, for they must explain the writer's point of view. An argument also seeks to prove that other points of view are wrong.

Arguments are most interesting when the issues are important and all sides are fair to each other. The questions that create good arguments arise naturally as historians do research, weigh evidence, and make judgments that may not persuade others. Was Christianity, as Edward Gibbon held in the eighteenth century, a major cause for the decline and fall of the Roman Empire? Did Al Smith lose the presidential election of 1928 to Herbert Hoover because he was a Catholic? Was British insensitivity to the dietary rules of their subjects a principal cause of the Indian Mutiny? Have the poor of Cuba been better or worse off under the communist dictatorship of Fidel Castro than they were under Fulgencia Batista, the dictator Castro replaced?

The writing of history abounds with arguments about what happened and why. They arise because the evidence can be interpreted in different ways according to the assumptions of the historians themselves. Sometimes such arguments go on for years, then they die down and smolder awhile, only to flame up again. Did President Harry S. Truman drop atom bombs on Japan because he feared an invasion of the Japanese home islands by American troops would result in a million American casualties? Or did he know that the Japanese were already defeated and eager to surrender, and did he drop the bombs because he wanted to demonstrate the weapon to the dangerous Russians who, he recognized, would be the major foes to the United States after the war? The controversy over these questions raged for a time in the 1960s, died down, and have received attention again more recently.

In any important historical issue, you will find disagreement among historians. The disagreements are valuable in that they discourage becoming frozen in an intolerance of opposition, and debates may make actually encourage toleration in the present. The disagreements also help readers see the sources in a different light. Disagreements thrive in book reviews. A historian who disagrees with another may make a counterargument to a book the reviewer thinks is incorrect. Jacob Burckhardt's *Civilization of the Renaissance in Italy,* published in 1860, has provoked a virtual library of response: reviews, articles, and even books arguing that he was right or wrong in his interpretation of the Renaissance—or arguing that he was partly right and partly wrong. Frederick Jackson Turner's thesis concerning the role of the frontier in U.S. history has been similarly provocative.

Stay tuned to your own thoughts when you read sources. Where do arguments seem weak? Where do you feel uneasy about your own arguments? Can you see another conclusion in the evidence? Often good argument is a matter of common sense: Can you believe that something might have happened the way a writer tells you it happened? Many people who hated Franklin D. Roosevelt argued that he knew about the Japanese attack on Pearl Harbor in 1941 before it happened but kept it secret because he wanted the United States to go to war. Such a conspiracy would have involved dozens if not thousands of people—those who had broken the Japanese secret code for sending messages to the military and diplomats, those who monitored Japanese broadcasts, those who translated them and took the translations to the White House and the State Department, and the officials to whom they all reported. Is it plausible that such a vast conspiracy could have taken place without anyone ever stepping forward to talk about it, especially since any such report could have earned millions of dollars in book contracts? Experience with human beings and their apparently uncontrollable yearning to tell secrets would seem to indicate that the answer to such a question would be no.

Good arguments, though, are founded on skepticism. Come to history as a doubter. Study the evidence over and over. Read what other historians have said. See what the sources say. Listen to your own uneasiness. Do not take anything for granted. And when you decide to argue, be as careful—and as civil—as possible. If you follow some simple suggestions you can enhance your ability to make convincing arguments. Consider them carefully and keep them in mind as you write and when you read the arguments of others.

Always state your argument concisely and as early and quickly as possible in your essay. You will help yourself in making an argument if you state your premises early, shortly after telling us what your argument is going to be. *Premises* are assumptions on which your arguments are based. In writing about history, you may assume that some sources are reliable and some are not, and you will base your argument accordingly. You must then explain why you think one source is more reliable than another. Having done so, you can move toward your argument based on the premise of reliability.

When you make an assertion essential to your case, always provide some examples as evidence. A general statement followed by concrete reference to the evidence provides readers reason to believe you. Here are excerpts of three paragraphs from a recent article arguing that ideas and images of eastern China and Manchuria helped fuel twentieth-century Japanese imperialism. Thomas David DuBois makes the case that these ideas had a long history in Japanese ethnographic studies.

> The interest shown by Japanese scholars in the villages of Manchuria is at least partially a legacy of native ethnography as it appeared in Japan. During the Edo period (1603–1867), travelers and scholars wrote accounts of Japanese local customs, both for the popular book trade

and with the aim of rediscovering a lost Japanese spirit, as with the work of the nativist scholar Motoori Norinaga (1730–1801). While much of his early work was episodic, a few attempts were made to systematically collect information on local customs, rites of passage, and annual festivals throughout the nation, and some employed surprisingly advanced methods, such as the 1813 distribution of questionnaires on local customs to each province, which demonstrated an embryonic attempt to integrate the local into a transcendent whole. Following the Meiji Restoration in 1868, a number of influences drove this interest in local customs to focus specifically on village society. First, many of the cultural reform initiatives of the early Meiji, specifically the eradication of popular "old customs" (*kyūkan*) and Buddhist practice, and establishment of an orthodoxy of Shintō ritual, required action at the village level. . . . Toward the end of the nineteenth century, the backlash against local Buddhism and the initial enthusiasm for Shintō orthodoxy and for Western modernism had begun to subside. However, researchers retained an interest in village customs, inspired now by the disciplinary mission of "salvage anthropology," and a common fixation on discovering the true and transcendent essence of Japan in its remote and unsullied countryside.

These ideas coalesced and matured in the work of Yanagita Kunio (1875–1962), the scholar most often credited with the foundation of ethnography as an academic discipline in Japan. . . . For Yanagita, the material and psychological life of the village, rather than that of region or family, was the cellular component of the national spirit of Japan, and as such the study of village religion would be foundational to any ethnographic project.

Yanagita and his style of ethnography . . . profoundly influenced a generation of scholars, including Ōmachi Tokuzō (1901–1970), who conducted field research in Manchukuo under the auspices of the Japanese military through the war years.[12]

Here is a standard pattern in historical writing, one that you can find in many articles from leading historical journals. Follow it

---

[12] Thomas David DuBois, "Local Religion and the Imperial Imaginary: The Development of Japanese Ethnography in Occupied Manchuria," *The American Historical Review* 111 (2006): 58–59. We have omitted Professor DuBois's footnotes and citations of his sources.

whenever you can. The writer makes a general statement: "The interest shown by Japanese scholars in the villages of Manchuria is at least partially a legacy of native ethnography as it appeared in Japan." Then he offers a summary of the evidence (with a very brief exposition of the views he mentions). A reader will be inclined to believe the general statement because the author has provided specific evidence for it.

Also, always give the fairest possible treatment to those against whom you may be arguing. Never distort the work of someone who disagrees with your position. Such distortions are cowardly and unfair, and if you are found out, readers will reject you and your work, the good part along with the bad. Treat your adversaries as erring friends, not as foes to be slain, and you will always be more convincing to the great mass of readers who want writers to be fair and benign in argument. The most effective scholarly arguments are carried on courteously and without bitterness or anger. When you argue, you would do well to remember the admonition of the Prophet Isaiah: "In quietness and confidence shall be your strength."

Likewise, always admit weakness in your argument and acknowledge those facts that opponents might raise against your position. If you deny obvious truths about the subject of your argument, knowledgeable readers will see what you are doing and will lose confidence in your sense of fairness. Most arguments have a weak point somewhere. Otherwise there would be no argument. If you admit the places where your argument is weak and consider counterarguments fairly, giving your reasons for rejecting them, you will build confidence in your judgments among readers. You may concede that some evidence stands against your proposition. But you may then argue either that evidence is not as important or as trustworthy as the evidence you adduce for your point of view, or that the contrary evidence has been misinterpreted. In either case you acknowledge that you know about the contrary facts, and you rob your foes of seeming to catch you in ignorance.

Always stay on the subject of your argument throughout your essay. If you do not, your argument could be submerged in meaningless detail. Inexperienced writers sometimes try to throw everything they know into an essay as if it were a soup—the more ingredients the better. They have worked hard to gather the information. They find their sources interesting. They want readers to see how much work they have done, how much they know. So they pad essays with much information irrelevant to the topic at hand. Sometimes they begin with pages and pages of background information and get into their argument only after they have bewildered readers with a story that does not need to be told.

Most importantly, you should take the advice of Barbara Tuchman we quoted at the beginning of this chapter and resist being "beguiled down fascinating byways and sidetracks" only marginally related to your topic. Get to your point. Trust your readers. Moreover, trust yourself. Make your arguments economical. Do as much as you can in as few words as possible. As you follow these suggestions for writing an essay espousing your point of view on a historical subject, here are some questions to ask yourself about an argument you have advanced.

Writer's Checklist

_____ ✔ Is this subject worth arguing about?
_____ ✔ Have I gathered enough evidence and used it accurately to make my argument?
_____ ✔ Do I represent the opposing views in ways that are fair?
_____ ✔ Have I developed my argument logically?
_____ ✔ Have I tried to prove too much?

Thinking about these four basic modes of writing will help you define more precisely your reason for writing an essay. Too frequently in history courses, students start writing without having any idea of the point they finally want to make about a topic. The instructor says, "Write a ten-page paper," and the student thinks only, "I must fill up ten pages." Well, you can fill up ten pages by copying the telephone book, but that would not be a good paper in a history course. Or you may have an essay question on an exam, but merely writing all you can remember about the course would not likely result in a reasonable essay. Thinking about the modes will clarify your writing task. It will also help your readers understand your purposes quickly. One of the hardest tasks an instructor faces is to read four or five pages into an essay before beginning to understand what the topic is. Help your hardworking instructor—and thereby help yourself—by writing essays in which your command of the modes of writing will make your purposes clear.

GATHERING INFORMATION

. . .

All writing is hard work if it is done well, and writing history has some special problems. It is sometimes easy to assume that simply being familiar with life—or some particular aspect of human interactions—is sufficient. George F. Kennan, the American diplomat and historian, confessed to making this assumption when he accepted the 1957 National Book Award for his *Russia Leaves the War:*

> I am afraid that I took up the historian's task somewhat casually, never doubting that it would be easier to tell about diplomacy than to conduct it—and not nearly so great a responsibility. But as this work gradually wrought its discipline upon me, I was both surprised and sobered to realize not only how difficult but also how important it was.[1]

Few people will be as honored for writing history as Kennan, but most can learn to do it successfully—and thereby learn to do other writing well, too. The problems of gathering evidence, analyzing it, organizing it, and presenting it in a readable form are part of many writing tasks in the world of business, government, and the professions that include law, engineering, and others. So you should expect to use your skills developed in writing history essays in whatever your future career may be.

---

[1] Quoted in *The National Book Award: Writers on Their Craft and Their World* (New York: Book-of-the-Month Club, 1990), 18.

All writers use some sort of process—a series of steps that lead them from discovering and refining a subject to writing a final draft. Different writers work according to different rituals. The two of us developed somewhat different ways of approaching our own writing. And we certainly recognize that in the nearly two decades since this *Short Guide* first appeared changes in the academic world—most especially in the areas of electronic technologies—have brought about changes in our writing habits. Many of those changes have made aspects of the work somewhat easier. But we are also convinced these changes have, as well, made some writing tasks more difficult. Overall, we remain convinced that good writing is hard work, involves some long-standing principles, and, above all, requires patience and practice.

Eventually you will find your own way of doing things. In this and the next chapter, we will walk you through some common stages of the work writers of history must undertake on their way to creating essays or books. At the outset, though, we want to make clear this is seldom a linear process—one step following categorically after another—leading directly to a written product. One step may instead take you back to reexamine what you have previously done; only then will you be able to finish the task at hand. Even after you have gathered, analyzed, and organized your information, writing the complete essay will likely take you back to those steps as well. The following suggestions may help you by showing how others write, but in the end you must develop the writing process that suits you best.

FOCUSING ON YOUR TOPIC

Most history essays begin with an assignment. In college courses your assignments will usually be outlined in the syllabus the instructor passes out at the beginning of the course or in the questions asked on essay examinations. You should always read each assignment with great care, looking for an indication of the kind of topic your instructor wants you to write about, the evidence she wants you to use, and the length the paper should be. Follow those instructions carefully. The topic may be general within the limits of the course: "You will write a ten-page paper on a topic agreed on by you and the instructor." Or the topic may be explicit: "Write a ten-page paper on the reasons for the appeal of Lenin's 'April Theses' in 1917 during the Russian Revolution." In some courses you might be required to write an essay with more of a historiographic focus: "Alfred Crosby, Daniel Headrick, and Edward Said have all written books about imperialism. Write a ten-page paper exploring the differences in their attitudes toward modern imperialism."

Many college courses may instead—or in addition—require that you write shorter essays, either on topics written outside of class or in essay examinations. Often these shorter essays are on quite specific topics, and you should read the assignments carefully to be certain you understand them; we have some additional advice concerning such essays in Appendix B. But many assignments in history courses—even on essay tests and for short essays—are more general. For many students, finding a topic in such circumstances is an ordeal. Professional historians frequently have the same problem, so don't be discouraged in your search. The ability to find your own topic reflects both how well you know the material and how you think about it. Defining your own topic is good discipline. A liberal arts education—including education in history—should teach you to ask questions and ponder meanings in every text and topic you encounter in life. Asking questions, and then still more questions, is an essential part of all your historical writing.

You should be curious about people, events, documents, or problems considered in your courses. This curiosity should cause you to pose some questions naturally, and especially about topics related in some way to what you are studying. For example, in one course you might study the Russian Revolution of 1917, in another the American obsession with the dangers of Communism and the Soviet Union during the Cold War, while in a third the music of Sergey Prokofiev. In studying and reading about any of these subjects your curiosity might well lead you to thinking about the half century history of the Soviet Union and its collapse in just a matter of months, something unforeseen (if sometimes hoped for!) by very few responsible persons. That amazing event should stimulate multitudes of questions you might ask to satisfy your curiosity about how such a thing could happen. And any number of those questions could well lead to an excellent topic for a history essay.

As you read and attend class, you can help yourself by keeping notes in which you not only jot down what you learn, but also the questions that occur to you, including—and perhaps especially—those without obvious answers. Keep a systematic record of all these questions, perhaps in a separate section of your class notebook. Or you might even keep a small, separate notebook—or a special computer file—entirely for these ideas and questions; a collection of such questions will have lots of potential paper topics in it.

And never be afraid to consider a well-worn topic. Why did the Confederate army under Robert E. Lee lose at Gettysburg? What qualities of Christianity made it attractive to people in the Roman Empire during the first three centuries after Christ? What was humanism in the Renaissance? At first glance you may think that everything has been said that can be said. Indeed, many things have been written on all these topics. But when you look at the sources, you may discover that you have an insight that is new or at least different and worth exploring. That possibility is especially good if you study a few primary source documents carefully and use them as windows to open onto the age or the event that produced them.

Sometimes you can find interesting topics in history by staying attuned to your own interests and experiences. If you are a religious person, you may naturally try to understand religious influences in the past. Do not use a history paper to convert someone to your own religious point of view. But religion is one of the most important continuing forces in world affairs, and it sometimes strikes us as odd that students do not think to apply their religious interest to exploring how religion has influenced historical events. The same is true of interests such as sports, food, fashion, and other elements of life. We have both sometimes wondered when the French love affair with dogs began and what historical significance it may have. History is a much more open discipline than it once was, and with a little searching you may be able to translate one of your own consuming interests or particular personal circumstances into a good research paper. One of our students wondered how she might answer questions from her children about the bananas they frequently ate for breakfast. So she did some reading, thought about the problem, and posed a number of questions; the final result was an excellent history essay on how bananas became such a popular food in the United States although almost none are actually grown commercially here.

We must, however, repeat an important axiom: Yours must be an *informed* interest. You have to know something before you write anything about history. Do not write an opinionated essay merely off the top of your head; your argument needs to be more than a restatement of your prejudices. Good historians read, ask questions of their reading, read again, and try to get things right. They try to think through their initial questions, examining the many facets of the problem and focusing on a narrower topic, one manageable within the limits of the essay they expect to write. You should do the same.

In our experience the most common flaw in student essays is the topics are so broad that the essays have no focus; their writers have not tried to refine the topics and cannot therefore develop an original idea based on the evidence. You cannot write an interesting and original paper entitled "Woodrow Wilson" or "Mahatma Ghandi" or "Susan B. Anthony." In 2,000 or even 6,000 words, you can only do a summary of a person's life—suitable perhaps for an encyclopedia but not for a thoughtful essay that tries to argue a special point. Very similar difficulties would apply should you decide to write on "The Causes of World War Two," or even "The Reasons for the Renaissance"; both topics are so broad as to defy any meaningful analysis in an essay of ten pages or so. If you can choose your own topic, pick a limited issue with available texts or other evidence that you can study in depth and write about within the assigned space.

Even if your instructor assigns a specific topic as the basis of your essay, it is almost always appropriate to limit, or at least focus, the topic further. Consider the topic we mentioned above: "Alfred Crosby, Daniel Headrick, and Edward Said have all written books about imperialism. Write a ten-page paper exploring the differences in their attitude toward modern imperialism." You will, of course, need to read the books of the three authors and determine the thesis each presents. Then you will need to compare the three views, analyzing how they are similar and different. These comparisons should lead you to a conclusion, and with it a specific argument for your essay "exploring the differences" in the theories about the causes and consequences of imperialism.

Whatever your writing assignment, or the general topic you first identify, there are usually ways to limit your topic either by narrowing its scope or adjusting your angle of vision. The scope of a broad topic such as imperialism, for example, might be reduced by focusing on the colonial ambitions of a single country. Even the scope of French imperialism could be further limited by considering French imperialism in the Caribbean, or even the island of Martinique alone. The geographic scope of your topic can frequently be reduced by also considering elements of time. You might consider limiting your consideration of imperialism to the period before—or after—the Napoleanic wars, for example. Or you might wish to consider the impact of twentieth century developments—such as the League of Nations or the United Nations—on French imperialism in the Western Hemisphere.

But in addition to limiting the scope of your topic, you might also consider changing your angle of vision. As we have previously noted, historians in this new century have successfully explored a much broader range of questions about the past. In this environment you have many more choices about how to refocus your topic. Years ago the usual concerns regarding colonialism were of grand politics or perhaps the details of colonial administration. You might also find occasional biographies of the key leaders. But with the changes taking place in the way historians observe the past there are many more angles you might pursue to narrow your topic.

You might ask questions not just about individuals, but about groups of people. How did French imperialism impact the various social classes in France itself? What were the effects of French imperial practice on the indigenous inhabitants of Martinique? Did French education policies in its Caribbean colonies increase the educational level of women as well as men? There are many other such questions which might well occur to you. In short, allow your curiosity to open new avenues of questioning as you consider your topic. Surely you will find several ways you might further narrow that topic so that you can craft an interesting essay with a new argument.

In the process of making your essay more focused, however, you also need to keep in mind that your topic must be defined according to the sources available. In some cases your assignment will do this for you; on essay examinations in particular, you are likely limited by the assigned materials you have read or heard about and discussed in class. But often you will need to determine what sources you might consult before completing your essay. We find it sad when students take this advice as a signal to limit their search for information. Instead we encourage them to search more widely and find whatever sources they can. And in the academic environment emerging with new electronic resources, there are almost always more sources available than you would imagine. Thus your challenge in refining and narrowing your topic should be simultaneously to expand your quest for useable information.

CONSIDERING POTENTIAL SOURCES

There was a time when our sole advice to students seeking potential sources for their essays was to go to the library. Of course that has become much too limiting an approach as the field of "library science" has itself grown to become "information science." Yet we affirm the advice in earlier editions of this book, that smart students and smart professors should learn to talk to reference librarians about sources of information. And it transcends matters of books and encyclopedias to encompass electronic search techniques and information retrieval and the evaluation of sources.

Several years ago when one of us was engaged in research about American westward expansion in the 1850s, a reference librarian at the University of Tennessee supplied the answer to a perplexing question: How might someone have amputated an injured arm on the Western plains at that time? In a wink she produced a little book called *Gunn's Domestic Medicine*, published in 1831. It provided complete and optimistic instructions which, as it turned out, found their way into a historical novel wherein one of the characters followed those very directions. Several doctors, on reading that account, have expressed cautious astonishment that a historian and mere writer knew so much about amputating arms. Perhaps the author flunked out of medical school? No, simply credit a good reference librarian!

Of course, putting the information from the source to use was the writer's achievement. But that was made possible by the intervention, in this case directly, by a person who pointed the writer to a potential source. It is up to you to seek out such resources and to ask for assistance when you need it. However, if you were to ask a reference librarian every single question that occurred to you about your topic, it is unlikely the results would be nearly so satisfactory. There is much you can and should do to find information before seeking help in your search.

Your questions will take on greater seriousness if you have already made some effort to find at least a few of the basic materials that seem relevant to your topic. There are a variety of means you should use to begin seeking potential sources. Increasingly these are found in various electronic formats, while others are still available in more traditional print forms. Even as we encourage students to make full use of electronic searches and information retrieval, we have often been disappointed that they treat such efforts as the full extent of possible sources of information. Historians, especially, should be aware that materials written decades ago—and frequently not yet available online or in CD-ROM compilations—are often

quite valuable in print formats, though they sometimes can be difficult to locate. Search for those that might be important to your essay.

By all means, you should read encyclopedia articles and other
reference materials to get a broad overview of your topic. If you look
up the same subject in many different reference works, essential
facts about your topic will be stamped in your memory. And don't
forget that old reference books are valuable for providing widely
held beliefs about topics when those books were published and
some—such as the eleventh edition of the *Britannica,* published in
1911—are justly famous for the quality of their entries. Your library
reference room will have standard, multivolume general encyclopedias and single-volume reference works such as *The New Columbia
Encyclopedia* (one of our favorites). Many encyclopedias are also
available in digital formats through electronic networks in your
library and on the Internet, as is the *Britannica* eleventh edition, at
http://www.1911encyclopedia.org/.

Beware of the temptations offered by some online encyclopedias and Web sites parading as democratic reference sources. Among
these, Wikipedia, at www.wikipedia.org, is well known for having
more than a million separate entries in English and hundreds of
thousands in other languages. Anyone can contribute—and edit—
any entry, an effort to open scholarship on a "democratic" basis.
Understandably, this approach has opened up the possibility for
cases of incorrect (and even libelous) entries made and altered on
this Web site. While a small army of volunteers checks many of the
entries for accuracy and removes the most egregious, you can never
depend on Wikipedia for consistent information. As with some
other open-source sites, the entries may change from one day to the
next. While you may find Wikipedia an interesting place to begin
your research, you should look for more consistently verifiable
sources of evidence for your essays.

Also look for reference materials that specifically address your
field of inquiry, both on the World Wide Web and in encyclopedias,
dictionaries, and other reference books available in your library. Not
only broad fields of study such as art or music, but also historical

specialties such as colonialism or even the history of peace and peace-making are considered in valuable reference works. One we consult often is the seven-volume *New Dictionary of the History of Ideas,* which provides information about ideas you intend to discuss in your history essays. (The original five-volume *Dictionary of the History of Ideas,* published in the 1970s but now out of print, is available at http://etext.virginia.edu/DicHist/dict.html). Likewise, we often consult *Brewer's Dictionary of Phrase and Fable,* available in many editions since 1870 (the 1898 American edition is available online at http://www.bartleby.com/81/), and the much more recent *Dictionary of Historical Allusions and Eponyms,* compiled by Dorothy Auchter, as a starting point for thinking and writing about all sorts of historical questions.

If you choose a topic related to religion, you might consult *The New Catholic Encyclopedia,* a fifteen-volume reference that contains a treasury of information on religious figures and religious movements of all sorts. (The original *Catholic Encyclopedia,* published in 1915, is online at http://www.newadvent.org/cathen/). *The New Standard Jewish Encyclopedia* provides a similar source for the history of the Jewish people and Judaism. (The earlier *Jewish Encyclopedia,* published between 1901 and 1906, is available at http://www.jewishencyclopedia.com). There are many other reference works devoted to a wide variety of topics and many more are published each year. It is the job of reference librarians to be familiar with many of these; take advantage of their knowledge (and that of your instructors) and follow their suggestions about reference resources that may be available for your use.

If your topic involves prominent individuals, you should consult one of the many biographical directories created for both broad and more narrow subjects of study. The *Dictionary of National Biography* is indispensable for any work on British history. *The Dictionary of American Biography* is inferior and sometimes disappointing, but you can find there interesting information about important Americans who may be subjects of historical research. Many librarians have old nineteenth-century biographical encyclopedias, and these are not to be scorned although the articles are nearly always laudatory, and it seems as if the people—nearly all of them men—paid in some way to have their names included, perhaps by buying the books.

Do not hesitate to use reference works in foreign languages. Even if you do not read the language or don't read it well, you may locate illustrations, maps or other useful materials. If you have had a year or two of study in the language, you may discover that you can read the articles far better than you suspected. That discovery may draw you into further use of the language, an advantage to any student of history and essential to advanced work in most historical fields. Some of the articles you find—as is true of many reference works in English—will have brief bibliographies at the end listing standard works where you can find more detailed information on a subject.

Among the most important reference resources for historians are bibliographies on a huge variety of topics, some compiled by scholars specifically as reference works and others included by historians in their books and articles. Often you will find numerous bibliographies in library reference collections, and you may frequently locate others using library catalogs by looking for or adding the subcategory "bibliography" to the subjects you are searching for. There are a number of valuable general bibliographies as well. Be sure, for example, you consult the widely available *American Historical Association Guide to Historical Literature,* now in its third edition, edited by Mary Beth Norton and Pamela Gerardi. These two large volumes are a rich mine of information about books and articles on every aspect of history throughout the world. You may also find some specialized bibliographic references on the World Wide Web. A few bibliographies are annotated—that is, the compiler offers a brief comment on the books, articles, and other materials cited. It is possible the writer may judge some sources too harshly, some too generously. But such a bibliography usually provides worthwhile information about the contents of books and articles.

In addition to the bibliographies prepared by scholars, you should also consult a variety of indexing materials to build your own list of potential sources. Among the most valuable are indexes which will help you locate articles in magazines and scholarly journals. Most of these have their origins in the venerable *Readers' Guide to Periodical Literature,* which has been regularly published since 1900. Updates appear throughout the year, and at the end of each year a large, comprehensive edition is published. The *Readers' Guide* surveys only magazines intended for a general audience. Don't scorn this purpose. Although you will not find articles published in the specialized journals intended for professional historians, you may find interesting, well-written articles by important specialists by consulting the *Readers' Guide.*

In recent years many such indexes have moved to electronic formats. This has been a boon to writers, as often a single search, using well-chosen keywords, may yield a large number of entries for scrutiny. It is likely your library has arranged for access to several such databases. Yet few of those electronic indexes include more than just a few years of index results; most do not include materials published prior to the 1980s. So you will want to ascertain the chronological limitations of a particular electronic index and then consult the bound volumes of previous years, if they are available. Only then can you be confident you have made a thorough search for potential information.

In a few cases these electronic databases may also permit you to locate the text of entire articles. One that often produces quick results is JSTOR, The Scholarly Journal Archive. You can search the full text of more than 150 specialized journals in history and other fields, covering the full run of issues up to five years before the present for most titles. And you can receive electronically copies of individual articles you wish to read for your research. (These will be sent as portable document files, usually known as PDFs; to read them you will need to have the Adobe Acrobat Reader installed on the computer you are using. This is available free at http://www. adobe.com.) JSTOR is available only through libraries that subscribe to its service; there are over 1,500 U.S. institutions (mostly colleges and universities) that currently do so, as well as nearly 1,300 others worldwide. Listings of subscribing institutions can be found at http://www.jstor.org. Without doubt, JSTOR is a valuable research resource, and you should inquire if it is available through your library.

Some libraries may also, or alternatively, subscribe to Project Muse, a service offering access to about 300 academic journals, in a diverse array of fields, available electronically. Its database is also fully searchable throughout the full text of all available articles. And if your library subscribes you can receive electronic copies of articles from journals selected by your institution for your research. As of this writing, though, Project Muse emphasizes access to contemporary issues of journals. For most of its holdings, it does have some back issues available, at least to the date when a particular journal was first available through Project Muse. But for most journals the database does not include all of the back issues, unlike JSTOR which has extensive holdings of back issues (for example, issues of *The American Historical Review* in the JSTOR database go back to its first publication in the nineteenth century!).

Many other electronic databases have thoughtful abstracts prepared by expert readers. Often using such abstracts can save you time, but you should be cautious in assuming they will always provide clear and complete indications of an article's content. Two such indexes are especially important for historians. Particularly strong for its coverage of world and European subjects, *Historical Abstracts* has appeared each year for many decades and in electronic formats since 1981. It pages, disks, and now World Wide Web files contain thousands of abstracts of books and articles indexed according to author, subject, period, and place. You can browse the abstracts for materials related to almost any historical topic. *America: History and Life,* updated annually, includes article abstracts and citations focusing on American history, and also an index to book reviews. It goes back to 1964 and, like *Historical Abstracts,* is a fabulous resource. Both of these are widely available in most college and university libraries; you should consult with a reference librarian about how to access them in your library. It may be that you will need to peruse bound volumes for earlier years of some such indexes and perhaps for all the years of other indexes.

Don't be put off by this eventuality, for ignoring such valuable resources will do little to enhance your essays; bypassing them can only keep you from finding potentially valuable sources.

Of course, you should also make use of the catalog in your local library. In many ways this is one of your best guides to material on your topic even though it is usually limited to the books and other media actually available to you in a particular library. In some ways that is an advantage, as those materials have been specifically selected for inclusion in the collections. You can therefore have some assurance that they have been included not on a whim but with a particular purpose in mind. So if you have not already done so, early in your quest for material on your topic you will want to learn how to use your local library catalog. Although there are a variety of systems in use by libraries to present their catalogs for use, most have similar features which allow you to search for materials by *author* and *title* as well as by *subject* or *keyword*. Keep in mind that for a library catalog, the *subject* usually refers to a uniform set of subject headings created by the Library of Congress, so using *keyword* searches may, at least initially, prove more fruitful.

In the early stages of your quest you will want to discover as many potential sources as possible, and all of these efforts will have led you to a large number of other possibilities—books, articles, Web sites, and other types of materials, including collections of primary sources. Take care to keep your *own* bibliography from the start of your research, even when you are merely looking for potential sources. By starting early, you will save yourself much grief. All too often students have come to us as they are completing the final version of a history essay asking for additional bibliographic information, including—on more than one occasion—the title of "that little green book" on their topic, or some other reference to a less than helpful description by which they have remembered a particular source.

Your research bibliography should include complete information about the books, articles, Web sites, reference materials, and other sources you locate as well as recommendations for further reading in the bibliographies appended to these sources. You may wish to jot down the information in a notebook or on small index cards. The value of cards—that they may be easily reorganized or added to as the numbers of your references grow—has been superseded by the capacity to do the same using a computer word processing or note-taking program. Remember, though, the hazards of fire and theft (as well as other threats to the results of your research and writing) do not respect either electronic disks or paper note cards more than the other. It is always wise to keep back-up copies of all your work and store them in alternative places. Keeping all the copies of your work in your car or dormitory room is an invitation to unexpected disaster.

Even at this stage, you have not done all the preliminary work necessary to help in creating your essay. You must still tap into the best of these sources to find the material that will provide your essay with the information that will give it substance. Now you must actually do the research! But remember our earlier advice. You may suppose that historians invariably follow these steps neatly one after the other. Not so! In practice, things seldom run so smoothly. Historians may begin with one topic, discover another when they do research, and change their minds again when they start writing. As they write, they may redefine their topic, and as they redefine the topic they do more research. Writing down such thoughts often reveals gaps in your knowledge. So you go back to your research to fill in these gaps. And as you do research you will find suggestions of other materials in what you read. Source citations supplied by historians in books and articles may suggest other bibliographic possibilities, and the names and details you find in what you read in the text of your sources may spark other ideas for research possibilities. You will then have to examine and analyze these newfound sources.

DOING RESEARCH

As you move from gathering information about potential sources to analyzing those sources, you must also evaluate them. Your first touchstone, of course, will be to see if they actually relate to the topic you have chosen. If you have carefully crafted questions about your topic, you should be able to dismiss some potential sources relatively quickly. In fact, you may discard some even as you are continuing to locate others. At this stage, the information you gleaned from reading encyclopedias and similar sources will be especially valuable in making those decisions.

If you are fortunate to have access to a large and comprehensive library, you may find many of the books and articles you have come upon are readily available. Some you may need to view in microform editions. Although these are not as convenient—nor as comforting to some researchers—as printed paper or even electronic versions, they do offer a form of access welcome to a patient historian. If you have not often used a microfilm, microfiche, or microcard reader, learn to do so. In many libraries it is essential if you wish to read at least some of the materials you have located. You may also have the option of requesting interlibrary loan privileges to obtain a book or article not available in your library. You may find that a good interlibrary loan librarian is just as helpful in your research as a friendly reference librarian. It has certainly been true in our experience.

Even as you move back and forth between gathering, analyzing, organizing, and presenting the information for your essay, you need to keep the evaluation principles of the historian's critical method in mind. First you must establish that all your sources are *plausible* and *trustworthy* and then if they are *accurate* and can be *corroborated*. These same principles apply if you are using information from historical journals, books from your library, newspapers, or even information you may locate on the World Wide Web. For some of your sources, using these standards may be easier than for others, but you will need to make that effort for all of the sources you intend to use in writing your essay.

Secondary Sources

Secondary sources, created from an analysis of primary sources by others, will be an important part of the information you will use to write a history essay. They are the work of historians, and others, who set out to explain the past based on what they have learned from examining materials created at the time, often by participants in the events. Those secondary sources you will be most likely to use in your research will generally be of two sorts—articles and books—although some may only be available in electronic form. Applying the historian's critical method is somewhat different in each case. For example, the articles you locate in major professional journals will have, for the most part, passed through a process of peer review. Other historians will have read the articles before they were published, applying the essential elements of critical method. Their judgments will be a good start to making your own.

This is particularly fortunate because literally hundreds of such periodicals deal with history. Some journals publish articles about particular facets of history—the Middle Ages, military affairs, science, art, women—or the history of particular parts of the world—France, Africa, the Middle East, Kentucky. Others, such as *The American Historical Review* and the *Journal of World History,* have a scope as wide as the discipline itself. An hour or two spent consulting the annual indexes of periodicals in their printed form or using the full text electronic search capacities of a database such as JSTOR can open your eyes to many issues that touch on your subject. And since the essays you write in a history course are more like journal articles than books, the journals will provide models of writing and thinking that you can imitate.

Books will also be among the secondary sources you have located, and many of those available in your library. Most will also have been subject to some sort of critical evaluation, if not in the publication process then at least in their selection to be a part of the library's collections. That should give you some comfort. But since you will not limit your search simply to books directly about your topic, you will still need to make certain critical judgments. If you are writing about Woodrow Wilson, you will no doubt look for books that deal with his times. You may consult books about World War I, books about the progressive era that he represented, books about people close to Wilson, and books about various issues in which he was involved. In such works you would look up the name

"Wilson, Woodrow" in the index and turn to those pages to see how Wilson is mentioned. You will need to satisfy yourself in each of these cases that what is written about Wilson is both *plausible* and *trustworthy* and that it is *accurate* and may be *corroborated*. If you can satisfy yourself on these counts, you may discover yourself on the trail of a valuable insight.

Book reviews may also help you in evaluating some of your sources. Many historical journals contain reviews of books and some indexes to periodical literature—including many that are available in electronic versions—can help you find book reviews. You should also look in *Book Review Digest,* which has provided a guide to published book reviews for nearly a century. In this specialized index you search for reviews by the names of book authors, usually in the years immediately after the book was first published. While the *Digest* includes some academic journals, it also includes more popular reviews for an intelligent reading public. But these sorts of book reviews may also contain valuable insights about your potential source. A reviewer will tell you whether the book repeats old information, breaks new ground, or contradicts received interpretations, and often whether the book is well written or almost impossible to understand.

While a growing variety of Web sites also offer more book reviews online, H-Net Reviews, which are found at http://www .h-net.org/reviews, are particularly valuable, especially for books published in recent years. Most of the scholarly networks affiliated with H-Net: Humanities and Social Sciences Online commission books reviews, and literally thousands of those reviews are archived on this site. Perhaps more significant, the entire database can be searched using keyword terms or other parameters you select. This electronic review archive is an extraordinary research tool.

Occasionally reviews can be fiercely polemical, displaying historians at their worst. But some books deserve to be attacked because they ignore scholarly evidence or present a one-sided view of their subject. More often, uncivil reviews reveal pettiness and sometimes jealousy, and it is unfortunately often true that historians with radically new insights into a historical problem may be pummeled by old believers who think the truth was discovered long ago and is not subject to change. Still there is hardly any better way to be introduced to the historical profession than by reading lots and lots of book reviews. You should by all means read as many reviews of the same book—especially among your potential sources—as you can, since different scholars will highlight different aspects of a book. You will often pick up information that you would otherwise miss and then be in a better position to evaluate the book as a source.

Increasingly there are other secondary sources besides books and articles—not merely similar materials posted on Internet Web sites—that you may need to consider. You will likely find others reflecting cinematic and also journalistic interpretations of subjects related to your topic. Historic events and characters have long been the subjects of film, both those meant to document what actually happened and those seeking to entertain by presenting artistic versions of the past. With the increase in the number of television outlets, notably The History Channel, as well as the easy availability of videotapes and compact disks, these cinematic versions of the past have become a much more common source of historical information. Almost all of them are secondary sources since they represent the past as seen and interpreted by filmmakers. Even the best documentary films—such as those about American jazz music, baseball, and the Civil War created by Ken Burns—are not themselves primary sources, but clearly the creation of skilled storytellers and film makers working with primary sources to present an interpretation about events in the past. And many feature films that have historical themes or topics—some fairly recent examples we have seen include *Munich* and *Master and Commander*—are intended to be faithful representations of times past even though historians frequently criticize them for numerous inattentions to historical detail.

In any case, films do provide a dramatic connection to the past, one which may especially satisfy our desires to visualize what we might otherwise know primarily from written texts. Moreover, they offer many people images which have a profound effect on how they read history essays. Thus films on subjects related to your topic can, and often should, be among the sources you consult as you prepare to write an essay. You will need to evaluate them, not judging them on the format through which they reach you, but on the same basis as we have suggested for other sources. Are they *plausible* reconstructions of the past, despite such obvious gaffs as the Green Dragoons in *The Patriot* wearing red uniforms; and is the history they present *trustworthy* even when it is based on discredited sources, as was Oliver Stone's *JFK*. Even though you may worry about some details, is the film generally *accurate* and, perhaps above all, can it be *corroborated* by other sources. Applying the historians' critical method to films will help you to see how they may, and sometimes may not, help you in writing your historical essay.

You may also look to other popular materials, such as newspapers and magazines, for secondary sources. Occasionally both types of publications will feature the analysis of a particular subject which will include, or may even primarily be, a consideration of the historical background of a particular topic. Perhaps because journalists ask similar questions to those historians use, many of these articles can often be useful in your search for sources. A few major newspapers, such as the *New York Times* and *The Times* of London have cumulative indexes to subjects and authors appearing in their columns, and their issues are widely available in microform editions. Others have searchable databases online, although often access may be limited to those who subscribe to the service. But once you have located—and evaluated—such stories, some may be very important to the essay you will write.

Primary Sources

Of course, newspapers may also contain primary sources, especially those accounts of direct observation of events by journalists or other writers. Materials in newspapers also illustrate that sometimes the same document may be used as either a primary or a secondary source, depending on the use a historian makes of the source. For example, an April 8, 2003, article in the *New York Times* by Dexter Filkins reported a "Warm Welcome and Stubborn Resistance" as the U.S. First Marine Division completed its advance into Baghdad, Iraq.[2] This article might be a secondary source for an essay on the 2003 American offensive in Iraq; but it might as well be a primary source for an essay on the history of "embedded" journalists, participating in a U.S. Department of Defense experiment with wartime journalism. Understanding newspaper, and other sources, in this way will help you differentiate between secondary and primary sources for your topic.

Good history essays should *always* refer to primary sources; you can do so as well. Be on the lookout for editions of the works by the various people who may enter your essay. Using texts written by those you write about gives your own work authority. When you use any edition of collected or selected works, check the dates of publication. Sometimes several different editions have been published of the same works. These editions may be of different sorts. The most valuable are editions of the complete works in which every surviving text is collected and indexed, sometimes with other materials from the time the person lived. These can be important to determine the different views of your subject either over time or when addressing different audiences.

Look for collections of speeches or sermons, published diaries, and editions of correspondence, all of which are also fairly common. Also read published (and, if they are available to you, unpublished) autobiographies, but be skeptical of them. Apply the same critical historical standards you would for any other source: Is the account *plausible, trustworthy, accurate,* and can it be *corroborated?* Remember, when anyone writes anything about themselves, they have a natural desire to shape the image of themselves for posterity. Autobiographies and memoirs almost always have a lot of fiction in

---

[2] Dexter Filkins, "Warm Welcome and Stubborn Resistance for Marines," *New York Times,* 8 April 2003, A1.

them. Still, all of them contain some truth—although some are more truthful than others. The recent furor over James Frye's memoir, *A Million Little Pieces,* and his apparent invention of many details has drawn attention to such problems. His defense, that the work contains "the emotional truth," was roundly criticized. Yet the problem is a real one, even for a historian writing a memoir, as Frank F. Mathias understood. In recounting his life as a young soldier in the South Pacific in *GI Jive: An Army Bandsman in World War II,* Mathias later confessed he used "my memory, my letters, and some imagination to present a true picture."[3]

Perhaps this is why most historians enjoy reading such sources. Like photographs, they give us a sense of intimacy with bygone times and people we have not known. And like photographs, the speeches, diaries, and letters are frequently datable. You can quickly see that they belong to a certain time and place, and in the eternal flux of things, they seem to make time stand still for a moment. Sermons and speeches can give you a sense of the public image and message someone wanted to convey. Diaries and collections of letters, on the other hand, frequently give us figures in relatively unguarded prose, commenting on daily life without the caution that marks more public utterances. The private persona or personality of the diarist or letter writer may be different from the public image displayed in speeches or writing intended for a large audience. But take note: The historian—rather than the former soldier—Mathias also cautions that in a memoir, just as in photographs, sermons, diaries, speeches, and letters, "imagination must enhance truth."[4]

Whenever you are using such primary sources, you will need to apply your standards of historical criticism. Are the claims *plausible* and are there reasons for you to treat them as *trustworthy?* For example, are you reading a copy of the letter saved by the author

---

[3] Frank F. Mathias, "Writing a Memoir: The Involvement of Art with Craft," *The History Teacher* 19 (1986): 378.

[4] Mathias, 379.

or one collected by the recipient? Despite the best of intentions, these are not always exactly the same. Keep that in mind, although you may have no choice but to use whatever version is available. Also consider if any claims or assertions made are *accurate*. Can you *corroborate* them from other sources?

Often numerous primary sources relating to a general topic are collected and published in a form that may be readily available. One of the most monumental of these is *The War of the Rebellion: A Compilation of the Official Records of the Union and Confederate Armies*, published in seventy volumes a century ago and now available online at http://moa.cit.cornell.edu/moa/browse.monographs/waro.html. The original volumes are indexed; however, the search functions in the online edition are cumbersome to use. A new CD-ROM version has better search options and contains additional related material. This vast resource almost seems to contain a transcription of nearly every scrap of paper exchanged within the armies on both sides in the Civil War, and there were many, indeed! The noise of battle during the Civil War was so tremendous that men under fire could not hear each other speak. Therefore written orders carried from place to place on the battlefield were much more common than in earlier wars, and thousands of these were collected by the editors.

We could list literally hundreds of additional examples of primary source collections that can help you in research, and many more of them are becoming available online or in other digital formats. Whatever your topic, check to see if you can locate a collection of documents related to your essay. When you search the library catalog, or use an Internet search engine, in addition to keywords for your topic, look for "sources" or "personal narratives" as an additional parameter; those are the principal terms used in Library of Congress subject headings to indicate primary source materials. Browse through the collections you find even if you do not at first see that they are related to your topic. You may be pleasantly surprised. But remember always to examine critically the primary sources that you do find.

Many museums, large and small, often have collections of historic objects that you might wish to use as sources for your essay as well. In the last few decades the number of such collections has grown tremendously. Many of them already have investigated these elements of material culture that can help you in understanding how they relate to the topic of your essay. But like every source you might wish to use, you need to evaluate them carefully. Not only must you consider "how people relate to objects," but also "the nature of the relation among words, images, and things . . . in particular historical contexts."[5] Rather than letting this dissuade you, consider it a challenge to expand your use of a wide variety of primary sources.

You may also find that your own college library probably has an archive or manuscript department with collections of unpublished letters, diaries, memos, and other materials. Look for them and see if there might be material related to your topic. There's nothing quite so thrilling as to look at the basic raw materials of history preserved in such sources. Many libraries and archives now also include oral history collections, tapes, and records of people—both well known and obscure—discussing the past and their participation in events. You can sometimes learn something by the tone of voice people use to describe past events, although other interviews may only be available in written transcripts. In either case, interviews are valuable for studies of recent or fairly recent history. If, for example, you write about some aspect of combat in World War II or Korea, you may be able to find veterans willing to tell you of their experiences, giving you a first-hand view of history. The same is true of the Civil Rights Movement in the United States, the Vietnam War, the Great Depression, the Jewish Holocaust in Europe, and many other events within memory of witnesses and participants still alive.

People who participated in great events or lived through particularly interesting times are often eager to talk about them. Don't be afraid to write or telephone people to ask for an interview, but

---

[5] Leora Auslander, "Beyond Words," *The American Historical Review,* 110 (2005): 1018.

respect the wish of anyone who wants to remain silent. It is always best, however, to conduct interviews in person. Prepare for the interview by learning all you can about the person and by writing out questions beforehand. But don't be mechanically bound to your list before the interview begins. Explore each question thoroughly. Listen to your source and be prepared to ask for clarification of details. If possible, record your interview on audio or videotape; if not, be sure to take extensive notes, clarifying and confirming any exact quotations you wish to record.

Remember, too, that primary sources can also include a wide variety of materials including photographs, material objects, paintings, sculpture, and architecture. Liana Vardi's fine 1996 article, "Imagining the Harvest in Early Modern Europe," considers representations of peasants by artists for three centuries after 1500. She shows that gradually the peasants, the farmers who worked the fields, disappear from paintings of rural landscapes. By comparing paintings with poetry from the time, she argues that city dwellers and aristocrats became afraid of peasants, who frequently rebelled against the harsh conditions of their lives. Then, in the eighteenth century, peasants returned to the paintings, where they appear docile and obedient and happy.[6] The paintings, reproduced in black and white throughout the article, serve as essential primary sources for Professor Vardi's conclusions about popular attitudes centuries ago.

You too may find important visual sources for your own essays. Yet do not be lulled into thinking that all images, and especially photographs, can reproduce reality as you might imagine it. Alan Trachtenberg understood and explained this nearly two decades ago in his article, "Albums of War: On Reading Civil War Photographs." The many, some famous, photographs of that war may have shaped subsequent images of the conflict, but they are, Professor

---

[6] Liana Vardi, "Imagining the Harvest in Early Modern Europe," *The American Historical Review* 101 (1996): 1357–1397.

Trachtenberg wrote, "vulnerable to exactly the same obscurities of other forms of evidence. The simplest documentary questions of who did what, when, where, and why may be impossible to answer."[7] We could not agree more, and once again encourage you to question *all* your sources and evaluate them carefully.

But at the same time, when considering primary sources for your essay, Professor Vardi's article should also remind you not to dismiss the possibilities of literature—poetry, short stories, and novels—which often capture the tenor and tone of the time in which they were written. While literary sources are sometimes difficult to interpret, particularly given the frequent metaphorical and occasionally personal expressions of the authors, in many cases the connections to a historical topic are clear enough. Consider, for example, this 1899 poem, "Take Up the White Man's Burden," by the well-known Anglo-Indian Rudyard Kipling, which he specifically headed "The United States and the Philippine Islands":

> Take up the White Man's burden—
>   Send forth the best ye breed—
> Go bind your sons to exile
>   To serve your captives' need;
> To wait in heavy harness
>   On fluttered folk and wild—
> Your new caught, sullen peoples,
>   Half devil and half child.
>
> . . . .
>
> Take up the White Man's burden—
>   Ye dare not stoop to less—
> Nor call too loud on Freedom
>   To cloak your weariness;

---

[7] Alan Trachtenberg, "Albums of War: On Reading Civil War Photographs," *Representations* 9 (1985): 2–3.

By all ye cry or whimper,
  By all ye leave or do,
The silent, sullen peoples
  Shall weigh your Gods and you.[8]

Were you writing an essay on United States imperialism—or on imperialism and colonialism in general—the importance of this poem as a primary source should be clear. These brief verses capture some essential expressions of the colonial mentality of that era and, if nothing else, could lend an added dimension to your essay on the subject. Frequently you may come across literary works, perhaps some not so well known as Kipling's, which can serve to enliven what you write. You might need to do some additional reading to make certain your interpretation is not too far from the mark. Consider that effort, too, a part of the evaluation process necessary before you use your sources for any history essay, and also as another example of the hard work that is required if you are to write well.

Writer's Checklist

_____   ✔ Is my essay clearly focused on the topic?
_____   ✔ Have I refined the topic so that it is manageable?
_____   ✔ Have I looked for all the available reference materials related to the topic?
_____   ✔ Does my working bibliography reflect all the available sources?
_____   ✔ Have I used the citations in my secondary sources to find other available materials?
_____   ✔ What primary sources are related to the topic have I found?
_____   ✔ Have I asked questions about and evaluated all my sources?

---

[8] Rudyard Kipling, "Take Up the White Man's Burden," in *A Choice of Kipling's Verse,* ed. T. S. Eliot (New York: Anchor Books, 1941), 143–144. There are many editions of Kipling's poetry available.

TAKING NOTES AND WRITING DRAFTS

■ ■ ■

Although every respectable historian knows the importance of gathering information before completing a historical essay, most also know how important it is to begin the writing process as early as possible. In reality, this is a form of practice. Pianists do finger exercises before they play. Baseball players take batting practice before a game. These activities help them limber up for the real thing. Similar exercises will help you prepare to write. Maintaining such a view of the writing process will also help you avoid some common, and often recurring, myths about writing.

One such myth is that writers are inspired, that real writers turn out articles and books and reports with the greatest of ease. Another is that if you must write several drafts of anything, you are not a good writer. Still another is that if you labor to write what you want to say, you will not improve it much if you write a second or even a third draft. We can well attest that none of these is really true in practice. While every writer has a different approach to the process, it is neither quick nor easy for any of them. All writing—if it is done well—is hard work.

For example, few writers manage to write without revising. The almost unanimous testimony of good writers in all disciplines is that writing is always difficult and that they must write several drafts to be satisfied with an essay or a book. The easier writing is to read, the harder it has been for the writer to produce it. Your final draft must express a clear understanding of your own thoughts.

But the way to that understanding may lead through several drafts. Writing, taking notes, rereading, and revising clarifies your thoughts and strengthens your hold on your own ideas. Once you have gone through that process, you have an essay that cannot be blown away by the first person who comes along with a firm opinion.

If you start writing early in the process, the great values of rewriting will be clearer to you. As you take notes during a lecture or discussion, do not let your writing stop there. Afterwards, write a brief summary of the important points made and also jot down any questions that come to mind about what has been said. That process alone may lead you back to update certain sections of your notes. It will likely lead you as well to formulate further ideas about what you have just heard. Such a writing habit may also produce a personal treasure trove of topics for future history essays.

It is also usually good to start writing soon after you get an assignment. Do *not* attempt to make this preliminary writing a complete rough draft. Simply set down your thoughts about the topic you have been given or—drawing upon the collection of potential topics you have already made—brief ideas concerning the topics you might write about in completing the assignment. You can begin by merely jotting a few words or phrases without trying to work them into paragraphs. Gradually, you may continue forming full sentences and disconnected paragraphs that allow you to work out your ideas. They, in turn, will stir your mind to more thoughts.

Inexperienced writers often assume that an accomplished writer simply does all the research first and then writes. On the contrary, most experienced writers find that no matter how much they know about a subject at the start, the act of writing forces them to confront new problems and new questions, gives them new leads, sends them off in search of more information to pursue those new leads, and eventually takes them to conclusions different from those with which they began. For the experienced writer, the writing proceeds in a process of leaping forward and jumping back, but above all involves some sorts of writing very early and continuing until the essay is completed.

To postpone writing until you have done all the possible research on the subject can be disastrous. Many historians have fallen before the demand they put on themselves to read one more book or article before they could start writing. That was the fate of Frederick Jackson Turner, who, after propounding his "frontier thesis" of American history, was expected to write many important books. He signed several contracts with publishers without being able to produce the books. Historian Richard Hofstadter wrote the following sad words about Turner. They should be stamped in the minds of every historian tempted to put off writing!

[Turner] became haunted by the suspicion, so clear to his biographer, that he was temperamentally "incapable of the sustained effort necessary to complete a major scholarly volume." "I hate to write," he blurted out to a student in later years, "it is almost impossible for me to do so." But it was a self-description arrived at after long and hard experience. In 1901 when he was forty, Turner had signed contracts for nine books, not one of which was ever to be written and only a few of which were even attempted, and his life was punctuated by an endless correspondence with disappointed publishers. For an academic family, the Turners lived expensively and entertained generously, and the income from any of the textbooks he promised to write would have been welcome, but the carrot of income was no more effective than the stick of duty and ambition. Turner's teaching load at Wisconsin was for a time cut down, in the hope that it would clear the way for his productive powers, but what it produced was only a misunderstanding with university trustees. Turner's reluctance to address himself to substantive history was so overwhelming that A. B. Hart, a martinet of an editor who presided with ruthless energy over the authors of the American Nation series, extracted *Rise of the New West* out of him only by dint of an extraordinary series of nagging letters and bullying telegrams. Hart in the end counted this his supreme editorial achievement. "It ought to be carved on my tombstone that I was the only man in the world that secured what might be called an adequate volume from Turner," he wrote to Max Farrand; and Farrand, one of Turner's closest friends who watched his agonized efforts to produce his last unfinished volume in the splendid setting provided by the

Huntington Library, sadly concluded that he would not have finished it had he lived forever.

Over the years Turner had built up a staggering variety of psychological and mechanical devices, familiar to all observers of academia, to stand between himself and the finished task. There was, for example, a kind of perfectionism, which sent him off looking for one more curious fact or decisive bit of evidence, and impelled the elaborate rewriting of drafts that had already been rewritten. There were the hopelessly optimistic plans for what he would do in the next two or twelve or eighteen months, whose inevitable nonfulfillment brought new lapses into paralyzing despair. There was an undisciplined curiosity, an insatiable, restless interest in *everything*, without a correspondingly lively determination to consummate anything; a flitting from one subject to another, a yielding to the momentary pleasures of research as a way of getting further from the discipline of writing. ("I have a lot of fun exploring, getting lost and getting back, and telling my companions about it," he said, but "telling" here did not mean writing.) There was over-research and over-preparation with the consequent inability to sort out the important from the trivial—a small mountain of notes, for example, gathered for a trifling projected children's book of 25,000 words on George Rogers Clark. There were, for all the unwritten books, thirty-four large file drawers bulging with notes on every aspect of American history. There were elaborate maps, drawn to correlate certain forces at work in American politics. There were scrapbooks, and hours spent filling them in. . . . There were, of course, long letters of explanation to publishers, and other letters setting forth new plans for books. There was indeed an entire set of letters to Henry Holt and Company, examining various possible titles for the last unfinishable volume— letters that the exasperated publishers finally cut off by suggesting that the matter might well wait until the book itself became a reality.[1]

Turner's life helps illustrate our fundamental belief about writing: at some point you have to settle down and do it, and doing it takes a kind of courage that every historian must summon up if he or she is to do the job.

---

[1] Richard Hofstadter, *The Progressive Historians* (New York: Knopf, 1968), 115–117.

RECORDING INFORMATION AND IDEAS

As we have suggested, you should approach writing as an ongoing process. Begin by actively listening and taking notes during class meetings. Listen carefully for important concepts, taking cues from repeated phrases, enumerated lists, and items presented in writing. Use quotations marks for key ideas stated briefly, but you should not try to take down every word. Instead always make an effort to focus on what is most important. After class, try to summarize what you heard and consolidate your understanding of the most important concepts. Write down any questions you have about the information; many instructors will entertain—in later classes or during individual consultations—your questions and attempt to help you understand more clearly what they want you to know. Write down those answers as well! This active note-taking process will be a great help as you study for tests and especially when you begin preparation for essay examinations.

Note-taking from your reading and research, however, will be even easier. As you are reading, you can go back and reread, concentrating on what was not clear to you at first. Always work on identifying the major points, separating them from supporting arguments and subsidiary evidence. Take extra care to use quotation marks for any direct statements you want to remember, but keep even those to a minimum. Always try to summarize in your own words. As an example, consider this brief passage from the well-regarded book, *Sweetness and Power: The Place of Sugar in Modern History,* by Sidney Mintz:

> When it was first introduced into Europe around 1100 A.D., sugar was grouped with spices—pepper, nutmeg, mace, ginger, cardamom, coriander, galingale (related to ginger), saffron, and the like. Most of these were rare and expensive tropical (and exotic) imports, used sparingly by those who could afford them at all. In the modern world, sweetness is not a "spice taste," but is counterposed to other tastes of all kinds (bitter as in "bittersweet," sour as in "sweet and sour," piquant as in "hot sausage" and "sweet sausage"), so that today it is difficult to view

sugar as a condiment or spice. But long before most north Europeans came to know of it, sugar was consumed in large quantities as a medicine and spice in the eastern Mediterranean, in Egypt, and across North Africa. Its medical utility had already been firmly established by physicians of the time—including Islamized Jews, Persians, and Nestorian Christians, working across the Islamic world from India to Spain—and it entered slowly into European medical practice via Arab pharmacology.

As a spice sugar was prized among the wealthy and powerful of western Europe, at least from the Crusades onward. By "spice" is meant here that class of "aromatic vegetable productions," to quote Webster's definition, "used in cooking to season food and flavor sauces, pickles, etc." We are accustomed not to thinking of sugar as spice, but, rather, to thinking of "sugar *and* spice." This habit of mind attests to the significant changes in the use and meanings of sugar, in the relationship between sugar and spices, and in the place of sweetness in western food systems that have occurred since 1100.[2]

Here are some notes taken after reading this passage:

> --sugar introduced to Europe ca. 1100 AD, grouped with spices--rare & expensive tropical imports, used sparingly by those who could afford them
>
> --now sweetness not a "spice taste," but compared to other tastes--"bittersweet," "sweet and sour," or "hot sausage" & "sweet sausage"
>
> --before Europeans knew of sugar consumed as medicine and spice in eastern Mediterranean, Egypt, & North Africa
>
> --physicians--Islamized Jews, Persians, and Nestorian Christians in Islamic world from India to Spain--used sugar as medicine, slowly came to European medical practice via Arab pharmacology

---

[2] Sidney W. Mintz, *Sweetness and Power: The Place of Sugar in World History* (New York: Viking, 1985): 79–80.

```
    --as spice, sugar prized by wealthy and
    powerful of western Europe since Crusades
    --Webster's dictionary: "spice" "aromatic
    vegetable productions used in cooking to
    season food and flavor sauces, pickles, etc."
    --we think of sugar not as spice, but of
    "sugar and spice"
    --shows significant changes in use and meaning
    of sugar, in relationship between sugar and
    spices, and in place of sweetness in western
    food systems since 1100
```

These notes, however, would be of limited value. They are nearly 60 percent as long as the original excerpt and little more than sequential listing of what appeared there; the note-taker does not appear to have thought carefully about the reading. Moreover, these notes often repeat words and phrases, sometimes pieced together in the same or a similar order, directly from the original but without the benefit of quotation marks. Using these notes in the preparation of an essay could easily lead you to being accused of plagiarism, an unpardonable sin for any writer. Much better if you tried to read the original passage, summarize its main points, and at the same time indicate in your notes—by using quotation marks—any key quotations that you might later use in your essay. Now consider this example of notes made after reading, and then rereading, the same passage from Professor Mintz's book:

```
    Mintz, Sweetness, pp. 79-80

    Sugar long seen as medicine by Muslim, Jewish,
    and Nestorian physicians in Islamic lands; became
    known in Europe after Crusades (ca. 1100) as a
    spice and was regarded just as valuable. Hard for
    moderns to see it that way: "We are accustomed
    not to thinking of sugar as spice, but, rather,
    to thinking of 'sugar and spice'." (80) Changing
    perceptions of sweetness also seen in contrast to
    other tastes: "bittersweet" and "sweet and sour."
```

Notice how this second set of notes attempts to capture both the historical sequence of events *and* the main idea of the original passage. These notes also indicate clearly, in an abbreviated reference, the source of all the information and, more specifically, the exact reference for the quotation. Taking notes such as these from the very beginning of your research will not only help you with information for your essay; doing so will also be an early start on the writing process. And you may well benefit from taking notes such as these as you read required texts in your history classes as well, not just for essay examinations, but also in being better prepared for lectures and class discussions.

As you read background information for any essay, you should certainly keep brief notes with location information, including URLs for Web sources and page numbers for books and articles. You may not write extensive notes at this stage, but the location details will help you find the information again should you need it. Write down questions about what you read, much as you would when you take notes during your classes. (We often scribble notes and questions in the margins of our own books. But never, NEVER write in a library book, or any book you have borrowed.) There are many ways to keep such notes. For years we recommended that our students take notes on 3 X 5 cards or keep a separate notebook for each project. Either are easy to carry in a briefcase or book bag, and we found them more convenient than loose tablets of paper. In recent years we have come to rely more and more on our computers for note-taking as well as writing.

Whatever format you select, the main point is to take notes even as you begin your investigations. Ask yourself questions (and as a part of your initial writing, while they are still fresh in your mind, jot down a few possible—yet plausible answers). Put down significant phrases. Note places where your sources disagree. Pay attention to what one historian notices and another ignores. Make notes of your own opinions about both the historians and the material. Even in the early stages of your research, important ideas may pop into your head. Write them down and then test them with further study. You may discover that further research confirms that some of your first impressions are gems!

You should keep a working bibliography in your notes from these beginning stages of your research. Take special care to include the essential elements of information for each reference you consult, recorded on a separate card or entry. Each such entry should include all of the following: *authorship* (and also the names of editors and/or translators); the *title* (or titles, in the case of an article in a book or journal); the *location* where you found the information (including the publisher and the place of publication or, in the case of Internet information, the URL, and—when appropriate—volume and page numbers); and the *date(s)* of publication and/or access. It is not necessary to follow the conventions for note or bibliographic formats as you begin, but it is very important to be sure you include all the essential details. For example, you might consult:

Adams, Ephraim Douglass. *The Power of Ideals in American History*. AMS Press, New York, 1969.

This information will need to be reorganized when you write in a conventional bibliographic or other reference format, but the first principle you should always remember for any note-taking effort is a simple one: *Be sure to record exactly where you got your information.*

If you make sure to record all the bibliographic details as you start with any source, you can later refer in your notes simply to the author, a shortened title, and the relevant page (and volume) numbers. If you were using Adams's *The Power of Ideals in American History* as a source in research about the origins of manifest destiny, as did Penny Sonnenburg for her student essay in Appendix A, you might write "Adams, *Ideals,* 67" (to indicate *Ideals* as the essence of the source title and 67 to indicate the page number). Since you must be able to refer accurately to your sources when you write, you must also do so when you take notes. You will save yourself much grief if you keep track of your sources carefully while you do your research!

The second principle for good note-taking is to avoid copying too much direct quotation in your notes. Writing down the quotation takes time, and you can easily make errors in transcribing it. You save time—and sometimes create your best writing—if you exercise your mind by summarizing or paraphrasing rather than merely copying direct quotation. You may wish to photocopy some pages relevant to your work if you must return the book before you write the paper. But as a warning, do not be tempted to simply stash the copies in a folder with all your other research. Instead, persevere and make notes while the purpose of the source is still fresh in your mind. Writing down ideas in your own words from the beginning is especially valuable as it opens your mind to the possibilities of how you might present the information when you begin to write your essay. And be especially careful when attempting to paraphrase that you do not slip into copying the original with only minor changes involving just a word or two.

As you read Adams's *The Power of Ideals in American History*, you might make a note summarizing some of his views like this:

Adams, *Ideals*, 67   **origins**

    provides background knowledge to understand the true beginnings of manifest destiny, not just in American history.

Notice the inclusion of a separate topic heading in the upper-right corner; this is especially helpful if you are using note cards, or in the margins of separate notebook. You can use such headings as you would keywords in computerized notes to find materials on particular aspects of your subject. When you begin writing your complete essay, you can return to the original source (or your photocopies) for additional details and quote exactly if that seems necessary.

But you might avoid that additional effort by keeping in mind the third principle for note-taking, which is to take special care in making copies of direct quotations. *Always* place direct quotations within quotation marks in your notes and review the quotation for accuracy once you have written it down. The eye and the hand can slip while you are looking first at your source and then at your notebook, card, or computer screen. It may help to put a check or asterisk (*) by the quotation to tell yourself that you have reviewed it for accuracy once you have written it down.

Here is a sample note of a direct quotation for an essay concerning manifest destiny, discussing the idea's historical beginnings:

```
        Barker, Traditions, 312        natural law/destiny

    *       The large and somewhat general expression
    "became a tradition of human civility which runs
    continuously from the Stoic teachers of the Porch
    to the American Revolution of 1776 and the French
    Revolution of 1789."
```

This quotation may seem a particularly apt explanation of natural law, although the words themselves may reflect historical writing of more than a half-century ago than it is to a direct quote addressing manifest destiny itself. Try to take such matters into consideration and use direct quotations only sparingly in your notes.

This may be easier if you also practice the fourth principle of note-taking, which is to make your own comments as you read and make notes. Commenting requires you to reflect on what you read, making you an active rather than a passive reader. *But be sure to distinguish between the notes that are your own thoughts and notes that are direct quotations or summaries of your sources.* We often put an arrow before our own thoughts whether we are using cards, a notebook, or our computers. The arrow lets us know that these thoughts are ours. If you do not take care in distinguishing your thoughts from the thoughts of your source, you may be accused of plagiarism, a very serious matter and one from which few authors can easily recover.

Here is an example of how you might write a note about your own thoughts on the origins of manifest destiny:

chosen people

➡   the belief in manifest destiny has mostly appeared to be a uniquely American characteristic, but further research on other countries and their "chosen people" concepts leads to belief that the concept of manifest destiny predated not only United States history, but in some cases even also predated United States existence as a country

The purpose of such a note is to keep your mind active as you read. Again, notice the inclusion of a topic heading which will lead you back to your own ideas as well as other information in your notes on the same topic; this will also help shape ideas for the essay that you will write.

ORGANIZING YOUR ESSAY

Taking notes that focus on both information and ideas—including your *own* ideas—will help you begin putting your mind to work organizing your essay. Having spent some time refining your subject, gathering a bibliography, doing spot reading, and taking notes, you should feel more confident about your knowledge. You will have left the somewhat flat and limited accounts of the encyclopedias and other reference books, and you will have started looking at specialized books and articles as well primary sources related to your topic. You should have asked questions along the way, writing them down in your notes. You will have noticed patterns or repeated ideas in your research, and you should have jotted down some of your own ideas as well. In these ways, your note-taking process should have helped you find interesting approaches to your topic.

Sometimes a pattern occurs in a consistent response to certain subjects. For example, the notion of manifest destiny was prevalent and commonly used outside the United States. Which nations also employed and extensively used this notion? How far back can one logically trace the idea of manifest destiny? You may have started with the resolve to write an essay about manifest destiny. If you were lucky, you thought of a limited topic right away, one you might do in ten or fifteen pages. Perhaps, however, you were not been able to limit your topic enough. Make a list of interesting topics or problems relating to manifest destiny. Keep working at it until you arrive at something manageable. The following notes illustrate this attempt to produce both something interesting and something you can do in the time and space available.

> "Manifest Destiny and its importance in world history."
>
> > --Too vague. Not focused enough with too many subtopics.
>
> "Manifest Destiny and its influence in European history."
>
> > --a narrower focus, yet still encompasses much.
> > --European history covers too large a span to incorporate into a paper of this size.
>
> "Manifest Destiny: The American Dream of Expansionism"
>
> > --too narrow does not recognize motivation for the topic, ignores the true question of its origins.

For this last topic, the temptation might be to go from manifest destiny to the American ideology of expansionism. Then you need to ask questions like these: Do I want this paper to be about the various stages of American expansion? Does this topic completely overlook the world influence of manifest destiny? Has my initial research been directed more at a global overview? In essence, What do I want to prove by writing this essay? What are other historical explanations of manifest destiny? As you ask yourself these questions, look back over your research notes and see if you can detect a pattern. Slowly an idea emerges and you add to your list of potential topics.

```
"Manifest Destiny: A Requirement for all
Nations."

    --widespread evidence of this, but still a
    narrow focus.
    --considerable primary source information in
    newspaper articles, plus Internet sources
    provide translated material.
```

Now you have a starting point, a provisional title. Remember, though, you can change anything at this stage, and your changes may be sweeping. While you use it, the provisional title will give direction to your work. That sense of direction will help you work faster and more efficiently because it helps organize your thoughts, making you evaluate information you have collected so you can make proper use of it. If you have done your research well, you cannot use all the information you have collected in your notes. Good writing is done out of an abundance of knowledge. The provisional title will act as a filter in your mind, holding and organizing things you should keep for your essay and letting information go that will not contribute to your argument.

Once you arrive at a topic, focus your reading. If you plan to write about the origins of manifest destiny, limit yourself to reading historians' explanations of the concept and philosophical works which underlay the concept. You may be so interested in manifest destiny that you decide to continue to seek more information about the use of the idea in American history to justify taking Mexican land with an eye even further south. Good! But while you are working on this essay, limit your reading to information that helps you to your goal. Maintaining that discipline will help you avoid the problems that plagued the famous historian Frederick Jackson Turner!

We would also encourage you to write at least a brief outline to help organize your ideas and your evidence.

Some writers sit down and start hammering on the keyboard without any clear idea of the steps they will take in developing their argument. Others worry about the details of formal outlining— Roman numerals, large and small, and the placement of each point or subpoint within the outline—just as they might have been taught early in school. But either approach may distract you from the essential task, appearing to be just another insurmountable obstacle to hinder you from writing. Instead, focus on organizing your thoughts. Most people find it more efficient to shape their ideas in some way before they begin to write a draft, and we have found that to be true in our writing. We encourage you to do the same, even for short essays and before you starting writing your answers for an essay examination. You can at least jot down a list of points you want to cover—a list that can be much more flexible than a detailed outline.

You can rearrange items on your list as your intuition suggests better forms of organization. Never be afraid to change a list or outline once you have begun. No matter how clearly you think you see your project in outline before you, write a draft! Writing may change your ideas. Be ready to follow your mind in its adventures with the evidence. Remember that you are taking your readers on a journey, not a laborious recitation of loosely related facts and information organized to read like an essay. You might create a rough outline something like this for a longer essay on the origins of manifest destiny:

```
Argument: John O'Sullivan's editorial about mani-
fest destiny leads one to believe that it was an
American concept to rationalize the expansionist
movement that was sweeping the United States during
the hotly debated annexation of Texas. But other
nations before the United States embraced the notion
in their own expansionist movements.
    1. John O'Sullivan's editorial itself is
       indicative of the selected people of the
       United States
```

2. Perspectives and explanation of natural law/right and how it can be related to manifest destiny
3. Early historian's viewpoints on the importance of using similar ideas in solidifying nationalism
4. Anglo-Saxon ideas of manifest destiny as essential for national survival
5. Global analogies
6. Early national precedents in the United States (up to 1840)
7. "Manifest Destiny" term popularized, 1840s
8. Extension to sea power and the Pacific Basin

A list outline such as this one avoids a proliferation of numbers and letters for headings and subheadings. You may add subheadings if you want, but you may not need them. Determining the sequence of your thoughts is most important and likely sufficient. Having made a list outline, such as this, you can more confidently write a first draft. In this case, you would have decided to shape an analytical essay looking at manifest destiny from a more global perspective. You will explain the origins of the concept, shape a narrative of its articulation and use, introduce explanations of other concepts relating to it, and explain why it is important to attempt to overlook limitations on the subject. Along the way you will explain who wrote about these concepts. And you can then actually begin writing your essay. Penny Sonnenburg used just such a process—of taking notes and writing drafts—in creating her essay, which you can read in Appendix A.

Writer's Checklist

_____ ✔ Have I recorded complete information about each of the sources I consult?

_____ ✔ Do I use my own words to summarize or paraphrase information I find?

_____ ✔ Am I careful to record all appropriate keywords in my notes?

_____ ✔ Have I taken special care, and used quotation marks, in recording any direct quotations?

    _____ ✔ Are my own ideas a part of my notes on the subject?
    _____ ✔ Have I looked for patterns, even unexpected ones, in the evidence?
    _____ ✔ Have I written out my ideas for potential topics and titles for my essay?
    _____ ✔ Once focused on a topic, have I created a list outline to sequence my thoughts?

WRITING AND REVISING DRAFTS

Leave yourself time enough to work on several drafts of your paper. If you start writing a major essay following this outline the day before it is due, stay up all night to finish that first draft, and hand it in without having time to revise it, you do an injustice to yourself and your instructor. You may get by, but you may not be proud of your work, and the instructor will probably be bored with it. A hard-pressed instructor, sitting up for hours and hours reading and marking papers from everyone in the class (and yes, we have actually done this!), deserves your best effort.

Note that we are not saying you should avoid staying up all night long working on your paper before you hand it in. Many writers discover that they get an adrenaline flow from working steadily at a final draft for hours and hours before they give it up, and they may stay up all night because they are excited about their work and cannot leave it. We understand that feeling from our own writing adventures. Hearing the birds begin to sing outside at first light before dawn after working at our yellow pads or keyboard all night long is an experience we have both shared, and we have liked it. That kind of night comes when we have worked hard for a long time, perhaps for years, and feel in command of what we are doing and want to drive on to the end.

But no writer can produce consistently good work by waiting until the last minute to begin. Discipline yourself. If you have difficulty starting to write, make a concerted effort to actually write for some short period of time, even ten or fifteen minutes. Then stop, consult your notes, take a break. But come back as soon as you can;

reread what you have written. Often reading over your work will stimulate further thought—and writing! Although you may not go very fast at first, try not to become discouraged. After a night's sleep, begin again. The most important task in writing your first draft is to actually write it! Get a beginning, a middle, and an end down on paper or on your computer. Write more than you need to write at first. If your assignment is to write fifteen pages, make your first draft twenty pages. Pack in information. Use a few select quotations. Ruminate about what you are describing. Ask yourself the familiar questions about your paper—Who? What? When? Where? Why? and also How?—and try to answer them.

When you get your first draft into being, several things happen. You feel an immense relief. An unwritten assignment is more formidable than one you have written—even in a rough draft. You have some idea now what you can say in the space you have available. You have some idea of the major questions you want to address. You know some areas of weakness where you have to do further research. You can see which of your conclusions seem fairly certain and which seem shaky. You can see if you have an idea that binds all your data together into a thesis, a controlling argument that resolves or defines some puzzle that you find in your sources. You can now revise and in the process eliminate the extra words and sentences you packed into your first draft.

Revision proceeds in various ways. If you write with a word-processing program, you can bring your paper up on the screen and start working back through it, inserting, deleting, and changing around the order of the paper. Many writers prefer to print out a draft and go over it with a pen or pencil, making changes that they then type into the draft on the computer. Some behavioral research has shown that the longer people work with computers, the more they tend to do their revising directly from the screen without printing out. You have to use the method, or combination of methods, that suits you best.

Perhaps the important part of the task is to read your work with a self-critical eye. You can cultivate a good sense of revision by reading your own work again and again. Be sure you consider, or reconsider, some of the steps you have already used in the process. As you read, ask yourself questions related to the six basic principles for writing a good history essay:

1. Is my essay sharply focused on a limited topic?
2. Does it have a clearly stated argument?
3. Is it built, step by step, on carefully acknowledged evidence?
4. Does it represent my own original work?
5. Does it reflect my own dispassionate thoughts?
6. Is it clearly written with an intended audience in mind?

Consider each question carefully as you read your draft. Reading aloud helps. You can sometimes pick out rough places in your prose because they make you stumble in reading them. Reading aloud with inflection and expression will help you catch places where you may be misleading or confusing.

Professional writers often have others read their work and make suggestions. Get help from friends—as we have for every edition of this book. Do not ask them, "What do you think of my essay?" They will tell you it is good. Ask them instead, "What do you think I am saying in this paper?" You will sometimes be surprised by what comes out—and you will get some ideas for revision. Also ask them what you might do to improve your writing so that the essential points you want to make would be clear to them.

Some of you may also be involved in a peer editing process in which students comment on drafts of each others' essays. Your college or university may encourage such collaborations, and/or your instructor may encourage you to do so. Or you may wish to form your own group—a kind of writing club—in which you will all help each other in revising your essays. There are also a number of explanations and guides to the process of peer editing, and many are available online. One that our students have found helpful is in the *Guilford Writing Manual,* prepared for students at Guilford College by Professor Jeff Jeske. Our students have retrieved it at http://www.guilford.edu/writing_manual/ by selecting "Peer Editing" from the menu. In addition, the ten questions in the Writer's Checklist for Peer Editing at the end of this chapter offer an effective approach you can use in the process.

If you do take advantage of this frequently effective approach in your revisions, keep in mind that the purpose is to help one another, not to demonstrate how much more you may think you know about writing—or the topic of the essay—than the author. Remember—a critical eye in the revision process is not just about making criticisms! As Professor Jeske cautions:

> It is worth remembering that a major goal of peer editing is to enable writers to make effective revising decisions. Praise alone will not help; when it appears unalloyed, it suggests that the editor has not invested the necessary effort, not thought deeply about the paper's effects and the way the prose could be improved.
>
> Nevertheless, the tone of the editorial response should be positive. Don't merely point out what's wrong. Identify the things that the author has done well: this way the author will know what to continue to do. . . .
>
> The collective goal is that we all improve—and, as this happens, that we develop a positive attitude toward the activity in which we are engaged.[3]

You will likely find that helping others with their writing will also sharpen your ability to improve your own drafts as you reread and revise them.

For most writers, the process of improving drafts goes on until the last minute. Writing and revising drafts will help you focus on all parts of your work more clearly. It will help you see your thinking, your research, your factual knowledge, your expression, and the shape of your ideas. Very often as you write and rewrite drafts of your essay, you will realize that your thought is flabby or you may suddenly think of contrary arguments you have not thought

---

3 Jeff Jeske, "Peer-Editing," in *Guilford Writing Manual,* http://www.guilford.edu/services/index.cfm?ID=700003980, (n.d., accessed 30 April 2006).

of before. You can then revise to take these contrary arguments into account. Reading your work over and over again, and taking advantage of comments from others, will help you track your own ideas so that they might flow from one to another without leaving gaps that might hinder readers from making the connections you want them to make.

Writer's Checklist for Peer Editing

_____ ✔ Does the essay stick to the topic and also deal with all the essential issues?

_____ ✔ Are the purpose—and the thesis—of the essay clear?

_____ ✔ Is evidence used effectively and documented clearly?

_____ ✔ Is the tone consistent and evenhanded?

_____ ✔ Are the author's views clearly evident, yet fairly presented?

_____ ✔ Is the writing clear, avoiding needless repetition?

_____ ✔ Are words used appropriately, avoiding clichés and needless verbiage?

_____ ✔ Is the essay organized clearly so that a reader can follow the argument?

_____ ✔ Do the conclusions mirror the opening in some way?

_____ ✔ What is the greatest strength of this essay?

WRITING IN AN
ELECTRONIC AGE

■ ■ ■

Within our lifetimes, the ways historians work—and write—have changed a great deal. The most significant of these changes, and the most obvious, is the widespread influence of computer technologies and their applications. While you might easily accept these technologies that seem to have always been a part of your life, a historical perspective on such developments is vital. "We should not perpetuate the myth that technology is a benign force," warns no less an advocate for the present electronic age in education than Vartan Gregorian, President of the Carnegie Corporation. His essential message, "that connectivity does not guarantee communication," is one you should embrace as a touchstone for your writing.[1]

Electronic storage and retrieval of information, an explosion of ideas and knowledge shared on the Internet, capabilities for nearly instantaneous communication over great distances, and a growing sophistication of word-processing tools for writing and editing have made what some believe are fundamental changes in the writing process. One frequent analogy suggests the Internet is the most revolutionary mode of communication since the invention of radio, while another asserts the impact of computers to alter the work of historians may even be greater than the printing press. To be sure,

---

[1] Vartan Gregorian, "Grounding Technology in Both Science and Significance," *The Chronicle of Higher Education,* 9 December 2005, B 4–5.

there are cynics, even among historians, who scoff at what they see as a naïve and all too prevalent assumption that everything useful is on the Internet. However, nearly all historians of our acquaintance do acknowledge the significant impact of the computer and the Internet on the study and writing of history.

A few even agree with the assertion that only when "historians begin to compose visualizations rather than write articles about the past" using their computers will they realize the full potential of electronic technology to transform their work.[2] Certainly historians have long seen a variety of visual materials—such as graphs, maps, charts, and photographs—as valuable additions to their written accounts. And the variety of electronic means for accessing and presenting them offers opportunities to enhance writing about and understanding of the past. Computers have, as well, greatly enhanced the analysis of historical statistics, including commercial accounts, census data, and voting records. But we are convinced, along with many of our history colleagues, that electronic technologies, for the immediate future at least, remain most significant to the greatest number of historians for their contributions to the process of writing about history.

But if computers have contributed anything new to the nature of history, such change "does not *fundamentally* affect the production of history," as the noted British historian, Professor Arthur Marwick, recently observed.[3] Thoughtful questioning, conscientious research, diligent evaluation, and careful editing all remain essential to historical writing despite the many ways electronic technologies affect each of these processes. We agree with Professor Jeff Jeske: "Writing is not simply a medium; it is a tool of exploration, a voyage of discovery, one that leads not only to new ideas but clearer ideas."[4]

---

[2] David J. Staley, *Computers, Visualization, and History* (Armonk, NY: M. E. Sharpe, 2003), 4–5.

[3] Arthur Marwick, *The New Nature of History: Knowledge, Evidence, Language* (Chicago: Lyceum Books, 2001), 146.

[4] Jeff Jeske, "Why Write," *Guilford Writing Manual,* http://www.guilford.edu/services/index.cfm?ID=700002920, (n.d.; accessed 1 May 2006).

Electronic technologies are a boon to that journey, though it continues to require the skilled work of all students of history to reach a destination yielding the stories about the past, intended to be true, which are the hallmark of historical writing.

So significant are electronic technologies to writing about history, throughout this book we have mentioned a number of ways computers, and associated electronic and digital innovations, can be of assistance in many of your efforts at writing history essays. Few of these are absolutely essential to your writing, but it would be unwise to ignore them if you have the capacity to put them to work in shaping your accounts about the past. In three broad phases of the writing process—inquiry, research, and revision—computer and Internet skills are particularly valuable. We believe they are worthy of separate consideration here.

INQUIRY

As you begin your writing process, thinking about historical puzzles and asking questions you wish to answer, the electronic world of the Internet can be a valuable tool. Indeed, the vast and still growing potential of the Internet and the World Wide Web may be the easiest means of finding out if what at first seem to be historical puzzles really are worthy of further questioning. You will be able quickly to find an astounding number of Web sites which mention almost any topic. Always remember, however, that anybody with an Internet connection can set up a Web page! As a result Web pages abound from individuals, from enthusiasts for this or that writer or painter or celebrity both living and dead, and from anyone with a particular point of view to promote. Naturally enough, various fanaticisms abound in this virtually uncontrolled electronic environment. If you want to post a Web page and maintain that you were abducted by space aliens who introduced you to Abraham Lincoln in another galaxy, nothing can stop you. Given the variety of American society, you will probably get a following who will tell you about their own conversations with Lincoln in outer space!

A popular twenty-first century source for quick information is Wikipedia, an online encyclopedia created in 2001. With entries on more than a million subjects in English (and perhaps half that number in other languages) written by two hundred thousand or more authors, this seems an ideal place to find something about any historical topic which interests you. Indeed, a recent report suggests it is among the twenty most popular sites on the Internet. Yet you should exercise an abundance of caution about relying too quickly on any Wikipedia article to answer even your initial questions about a topic.

Like the Internet itself, Wikipedia is open to all who wish to use it. Anyone can write an entry. And anyone else can edit it! This process may lead to collaborative efforts which enhance the accuracy of the entries, as the creators of the site intended. Indeed, some reviews by respected observers have concluded that on many crucial scientific topics the information available on Wikipedia is often more up to date than some print encyclopedias and contains fewer errors. But there is also potential for much mischief. Anyone with an axe to grind on some subject can alter information, and public figures often find that entries made one day about their accomplishments may turn into scandals the next, as opponents edit them in an effort to gain personal or political advantage. Such is the nature of the Internet as a democratic medium of communication. Of course, such electronic vandalism can be corrected, recalling Thomas Jefferson's admonition to his fellow citizens that "eternal vigilance is the price of freedom."

Despite problems such as these associated with open access to the Internet, you should not dismiss the Web as a tool of inquiry. Many valuable and important resources are available on the Web, and they are growing. To help you harness this potential, no doubt you will want to use one of the wide variety of available search engines to connect with Web sites containing some information on topics that interest you. The most popular, and some claim the most effective, is currently Google, at http://www.google.com, with a revamped Yahoo search engine, at http://www.yahoo.com, not far behind. Both attempt to rank the relevance of the results concerning your search keywords based on a secret formula, or algorithm, that evaluates how many links each has to other relevant Web sites.

Most search engines also prominently feature those sites whose operators pay to have their addresses advanced ahead of other search results. Sometimes these sponsored results are clearly identified, but not always. In fact, the operating parameters of most online search engines are frequently changing. This approach, some critics claim, creates a caste system in which some Web sites determine the popularity of others dealing with the same topics. This does not diminish the value of the search, but it should serve as warning when you move beyond your initial explorations to more serious research on your topic.

As you continue your initial inquiries, also remember that the advent of reliable electronic communications has made it possible for you to seek help from any number of historians and other scholars. Possibilities for discussion—through news groups, chat rooms, blogs, and instant messaging services—roar across the Internet without pause. Some may be of help to you as you ponder the issues about which you may wish to write. Their informal nature, often including the use of icons which may allow you to include visual clues to what you wish to say, make them attractive electronic places in which to consider questions about a topic. This informality has an important place in encouraging the kinds of questions that you must ask as you begin your writing process. And they may also offer excellent opportunities to begin writing at a time when you may feel bogged down and afflicted by writer's block.

Perhaps of more interest to those seeking answers to historical questions, however, are somewhat more formal discussion lists comprised of people interested in a particular topic to which the list is dedicated. Some, however, remain free-for-all forums where anything sent to the list is immediately resent to all the e-mail boxes registered for the group. Others are presided over by one or more moderators or editors who ensure that only messages germane to the list topic will be posted. Many in the latter group are of interest to historians, especially those sponsored by the scholarly collective known as H-Net, Humanities and Social Sciences Online. You can find the directory of more than one hundred H-Net discussion networks at http://www.h-net.org, where you can also access logs in which previous messages are archived. Although not all of them are strictly devoted to history, most do consider topics that have broad historical dimensions. They range from H-World, devoted to many issues in World History, to H-Quilts, considering the history and making of quilts, to H-Tennessee, with discussions and information mostly about the history and geography of that mid-south state, and many other topics.

All these H-Net discussion networks offer the opportunity to ask questions about many subjects—books and articles, puzzles in evidence, current problems—anything at all relating to the interests the group is intended to serve. Each has its own rules, including ways to join and ways to end your membership. We would offer one note of caution. A potential danger of belonging to several such groups is that your electronic mailbox may fill up quickly, and you might receive a great deal of information you don't want or need. When you join, however, you may be given an opportunity to set your options so that this problem is reduced, often by receiving daily digests of collected messages. Be sure to read the welcome message you first receive to discover how to do this. Such groups do form valuable scholarly communities, and you can tap into them in various ways not only to begin your own inquiries into a potential topic but also to eavesdrop on postings that may later aid you in your research.

H-Net discussions are somewhat more formal than the free-wheeling chat rooms and blog sites, yet they still remain informal ways to begin your questioning process. But as you develop your topic, you may also have opportunities to contact historians directly. When you read a book or article by a living historian, you may be able to reach that person by e-mail with a question and often receive in return a generous reply. The American Historical Association publishes an annual directory of Departments of History that includes a list of individual historians with e-mail addresses for many of them. Still others have e-mail addresses listed on the World Wide Web pages of the universities or other institutions where they are employed. Both of us have received numerous inquiries directly from students and through discussion networks to which we belong, and we have tried to respond whenever we could be of help. You may be fortunate to locate another historian similarly disposed.

As you begin such electronic discussions, remember the opportunity to connect does not ensure that you will be able to communicate. For example, the informality encouraged in chat rooms or as you exchange instant messages may not be the best way to encourage a serious reply. The great disadvantage of forming a habit of informal chat is that it can, if you are not cautious, lead to habits of writing that may be considered sloppy and ill-considered to serious readers. We recommend that you take advantage of the spell-checking features embedded in many e-mail programs as you finish writing any message, although you should recognize their limitations. Be sure to reread carefully what you plan to send, making sure you have been clear and will not be misunderstood. Such caution seems to some a betrayal of the open and democratic nature of the Internet that has been an important characteristic of this medium. It may be. However, the reality of written communication—even as viewed on a computer screen—is that adherence to common conventions of writing, including punctuation, capitalization, and basic grammar, remains of great value. And it is more likely to elicit a reply.

If your inquiries lead to fruitful responses from scholars, or if you have found encouraging information through your own searches on the Web or by reading discussion lists, be sure to take notes on what you have discovered. At this point you may be jotting ideas down on paper, but take care to organize them so they won't get away from you. A better solution is to take notes using your computer! We strongly recommend that you begin keeping electronic files with notes even at this early stage. That may be especially valuable later so that you do not have to retrace your initial inquires as you undertake further research. Almost any word-processing program can be used for note-taking and then be of enormous value in organizing your notes as you begin to write a draft of your essay.

Do take care—as you should in all note-taking endeavors—in selecting keywords and using them in your note files. You can later locate all of the references you have found on a particular subject by using the search or FIND function on your word-processing program to locate those keywords. Many such programs will also allow you to shift your notes into the electronic file in which you are writing your essay; simply block and copy text from your note files, then open your essay file and paste the information there. Be sure to indicate clearly [perhaps in square brackets] location information, particularly Web links or page numbers, as you write your notes into a computer file. For some Web sites, you must indicate clearly the precise and complete URL for the particular source you have found, as well as any search terms you have used to locate specific information.

While you may use most word-processing programs to accomplish such tasks, there are a number of specific note-taking programs that you might wish to use instead. A program we find particularly useful is Scribe, created by Elena Razlogova of George Mason University's Center for History and the New Media. It is available as a free download from the World Wide Web at http://chnm.gmu.edu/tools/scribe in a compressed file format. You will need to use a file decompression program to activate the Scribe program and its attachments before you can begin work; there is a link to a recommended program on the Web site. With Scribe, you can create virtual note cards with detailed location information, very long notes and separate personal comments, plus the capacity to use a large number of keywords. You can export footnotes and bibliography entries, formatted to match *The Chicago Manual of Style* suggestions which historians usually use. It does take a little time to study the instructions and master Scribe features and operations, although if you anticipate using it for several projects we think it will be well worth your time and effort.

Whether you use a specialized note-taking or database program, or merely take notes with your word-processing program, be sure to save your notes as you work and especially as you finish each research or writing session, no matter how short. Some programs automatically create back-up files, but we encourage you to make others. Take advantage of the easy means electronic media provides to save your work. Keep several copies using your computer hard drive as well as additional copies in other formats. For as long as we have been writing, we have heard disheartening experiences almost every year of tribulations students and colleagues have undergone because they have lost all their research due to one sort of disaster or another. We have not wanted to join them! In preparing each edition of this book, for example, we have kept copies of every chapter in a separate file, and have four or more copies of each—on our computer hard drives, floppy disks, compressed "zip" disks, CD-ROMs created with our computers, and USB drives (also known as memory sticks or flash drives) as well as printed paper versions. You should do so, too, even with the notes from your first inquiries into potential topics, and continue as you proceed with more intensive research.

RESEARCH

Once you have completed notes from your inquiries, you can continue the writing process by narrowing your list of possible topics. And then you can turn your efforts to careful research for the essay you intend to write. In connecting with potential sources for your topic, you will also find electronic technologies of great assistance. However, don't make the Web sites and discussion lists you have used in your initial inquiries your first choices for your research. Make it a habit to look first at the resources of your university or college library. You will find not only catalogs, most now offered in electronic and online formats, but also collections of reference materials as well as links to proprietary search and information resources to which you would likely not otherwise have access.

Although libraries use a variety of systems to present their catalogs for research, most have similar features. Online catalogs have become the most common and usually allow you to search for materials by *author* and *title* as well as by *subject* or *keyword*. Keep in mind that for a library catalog, the subject usually refers to a uniform set of subject headings created by the Library of Congress. You will have to enter these exactly for a subject search to be successful. Your library may have a collection of bound volumes containing all these subject headings, listed alphabetically. But it will likely be easier to choose the *long* or *full* catalog record of a work you have already identified to see what some appropriate subject headings for your topic may be. Easier still, you can search most library catalogs by *keyword,* usually a name or topic of particular interest to you. And most often you can also refine that search by either including or excluding other particular terms or specifying that a particular phrase should appear exactly as you have given it. Most catalogs have easy links to instructions to help you make such advanced searches. The results, however, will be only to materials that have been preselected for inclusion in your library. In some libraries, those offerings may be extensive, but in others they may not be nearly so voluminous.

Do not limit your initial search for material to just what is easily at hand. One expansive resource that may be available to you is WorldCat, a worldwide union catalog of holdings in about nine thousand libraries associated with the Ohio-based Online Computer Library Center. This is sometimes available for student access through member college libraries, although not all associated institutions subscribe for such widespread access. Nonetheless, a number of commercial associates—including some Internet search engines—do draw entries from the vast WorldCat database; information about these and an explanation of how you might use the service in this way is available at http://www.oclc.org/worldcat/open/default.htm. Another, alternative resource, readily available on the Internet for several years now, is an integrated online catalog of almost 12 million bibliographic records from the Library of

Congress; you can access it at http://catalog.loc.gov. The time you spend looking at either of these catalogs and studying their online directions and user assistance pages will surely be rewarded, sometimes with many more materials than you imagined existed!

You may also be able, either through your own institution's library or on the Internet, to find catalogs of other educational, public, or specialized libraries which you might also search for information relevant to your topic. If you find materials in a nearby library, you may be able to look at them there, or even in some cases to borrow materials much as you would in your own college library. But if that is not possible, consider making an *interlibrary loan* request for an article or book that seems to be in the collections of another library. Because Internet connectivity has made this process much easier and more widely available, you should certainly ask at your local library if it might be possible for you to make such a request. Don't be surprised if the result—especially for journal articles—is an electronic file to read in your library, or on your own computer. Still, all this takes time, even with the nearly instantaneous exchange of messages the Internet seems to promise. We have found that our students often underestimate the amount of time, and work, involved in the research process. In both general terms, and also against the possibility that you might need to await delivery of some materials, we strongly encourage you to begin research for your essay as early as possible.

Other valuable electronic research assistance can be found through JSTOR, The Scholarly Journal Archive, and Project Muse. Both provide full-text electronic access to scholarly journals in a variety of fields, including history. Project Muse has a database of mostly recent articles from about 300 journals, while the JSTOR database contains the full run of issues up to five years before the present for more than 150 specialized journals in history and other fields. Using either database, you can search the entire text of all the articles in the available journals by keyword or author. And you can electronically receive copies of individual articles you wish to read for your research. (JSTOR articles will be sent as portable document files, known as PDFs; to read them, you will need to have the

Adobe Acrobat Reader installed on the computer you are using. This is available free at http://www.adobe.com. Many university and college libraries subscribe to either or both JSTOR and Project Muse, and you should inquire if they are available to you. Most libraries do provide access to other electronic databases that can be searched for article titles, although few of these provide more than abstracts of content. Nonetheless, you should ask about these as well. With results from them in hand, you will be able to look for original printed articles concerning your subject in a library, or request them through an interlibrary loan service.

Many other primary and secondary sources for writing about history may also be found in abundance on the World Wide Web, some in less than obvious places. One historian recently confessed—if that is the correct word—to using the online auction site eBay as a location for research. Interested in popular expressions of northern sentiment during the Civil War, Jonathan White found several significant items for his research offered for sale by the "entrepreneurial junk collectors" among eBay dealers. White had not found these cards, covers, and broadsides through any database or Internet search, concluding that eBay offered "scholars a unique opportunity to consult or use items that they otherwise would never have discovered even after spending months searching through a multitude of library catalogs."[5] For some topics you might also find this to be true.

Although unorthodox, White's approach does offer a reminder that the nature of the World Wide Web is such that literally anybody can create a Web page and post literally anything for the entire world (at least potentially) to see. Many scholars applaud these developments as a further democratization of information. Certainly the role of a careful, and perhaps sometimes overcautious, journal or book editor is bypassed in the case of some Web sites. So, too, is the role of the friendly

[5] Jonathan W. White, "An Unlikely Database: Using the Internet Creatively in Historical Research," *Perspectives: Newsmagazine of the American Historical Association*, 44, no. 3 (March 2006): 53.

librarian, though many are willing to point questioning students to valuable Web sites as well as more traditional reference materials.

There are many listings, even entire books, of important or especially valuable URLs for college history students. These are designed to help you in making the necessary evaluations of Web sites as a part of your research process. In this *Short Guide* we cannot mention many, but here are several we have found to be especially helpful to students, not least because they all feature primary source documents for open public use.

1. *The Library of Congress*
   http://www.loc.gov
      In addition to its library catalog, The Library of Congress Web site is particularly significant for the large collection of primary sources on U.S. history available in its American Memory collection. And the more recently added Global Gateway provides a growing collection of materials and information concerning world history, including some primary source materials drawn from the library's collections. Both can be easily be accessed from links on the main site.

2. *World History Matters*
   http://chnm.gmu.edu/worldhistorymatters
      Sponsored by the Center for History and the New Media, this relatively new site is devoted not only to source materials but also to effective teaching and learning about history of, and throughout, the world. One exciting feature presents thoughtful, scholarly reviews of more than 200 primary source archives placed online in many other countries.

3. *Internet Archive of Texts and Documents*
   http://history.hanover.edu/texts.html
      Originally conceived as a broad collection of both primary and secondary historical sources, the Hanover Historical Texts Project was cut back in scope after July 2000,

with fewer entries than were once available. However, this new archive does include a link to the greater number of documents in the original Project files and numerous other Web sites containing historical sources. It is particularly strong for European History.

4. *Historical Text Archive*
   http://historicaltextarchive.com/
   First created at Mississippi State University, this archive moved twice in less than a decade. It continues to offer a superb collection of articles and books as well as more than 5,000 links to related material in many fields of history—as well as advertising logos, which became necessary to ensure its continued support.

All of these appear to be stable sites which you can depend on if you make citations to sources you find there. But the experience of the last two offers an important caveat about using the World Wide Web for historical research. Web sites are changing all the time, and almost any list of excellent Web resources may quickly become obsolete. Of course, everyone knows that books, too, disappear, not least by extensive use. And archives may be destroyed in catastrophic events such as fire or through neglect. But somehow the transitory nature of the World Wide Web often looms larger in historians' minds. The Web is not yet a substitute for a good library. Do not let this concern lead you to avoid using it entirely. Use the Web cautiously. Take full advantage of the powers of available search engines to locate potential materials. Keep good records of what you find. And always go back to any site at least one additional time to be sure you have recorded the URL and other information correctly. Also learn to recognize that some problems in locating—and relocating—Web materials may be caused not at the source of the Web site but somewhere in the chain of transmission to the computer you are using.

Strictly speaking, Internet (and other electronic) sources are not different from other primary and secondary sources. They do not really constitute a separate category of historical materials. You should certainly be skeptical about what you find, as you would when considering any historical source. In the case of World Wide Web materials, though, the role of historical evaluation has passed from such designated mediators as editors and librarians directly to the researcher and writer. In short, it is *your* responsibility to assess the value of the materials you locate on the Internet. Quite likely your instructor will expect you to "be more cautious and evaluative in an electronic environment"[6] as you prepare your history essays. This is not unreasonable. Nor is it extraordinary for any research you might do before writing a history essay.

If you begin the process of gathering information for your essay by establishing clear questions you wish to answer, you will be well on the way to an evaluation strategy once you turn to sources you find on the World Wide Web. Similarly, if you have done a little background work ahead of time, you will have a better basis of information to use in assessing what you find on the Web. Once you locate any potential source on the Internet, you need to explore the full site of which it is a part. Most high quality and reliable sites have easy navigation tools, not only on their home page but also on subsidiary pages as well. Try using these to see what else is available. Is it consistent with the specific information you have found? Or do the internal links take you to only marginally related material? If so, why?

If you start from a home page, such as that for the Library of Congress, try the various main links that you see. Discover what types of information you may find using several of them, then use the BACK feature on your web browser if you are unable to find a HOME link on one of the pages. Start your exploration again. Should you begin on what appears to be a subsidiary page, by all means look for the home page. If there is no HOME link available,

---

6 Deborah Lines Anderson, "Heuristics for the Educational Use and Evaluation of Electronic Information," in *History.edu: Essays on Teaching with Technology,* ed. Dennis A. Trickle and Scott M. Merriman (Armonk, NY: M. E. Sharpe, 2001), 135.

try following back the URL given on your web browser for the site you have found. Use just the letters and other characters beginning on the left of your browser's location bar up until the first single slash (/) as a separate URL. This may not always be successful, although it will frequently take you to the home or foundation site where the materials you have located reside.

Once you get to the home page, you will have to start asking questions again. Who created and/or maintains this site? What organization, if any, sponsors this work? Do they have any particular interests in the content? Or, are there no sponsors? Is this the work of a single enthusiast? Certainly individuals may create such Web materials for many scholarly or nonpartisan purposes. You may need to use the historian's skill of inference to answer some of these questions, at least in part. But if you are unable to locate any information about the sponsor or creator of a Web page, that should give you pause. Remember the high value historians place on skepticism in evaluation of their sources!

In this spirit, we also caution against an uncritical acceptance of historical documents, including photographs, which you might find on the Internet. Sadly, the creators of some Web sites have been known to alter even well-known historical documents (perhaps most frequently by omitting select portions of the text) in an effort to use the altered versions in support of a particular cause. And digital technologies have made adjustments in photographs far easier than it was in Stalin's day, when government officials of the Soviet Union disappeared from official photos of the national leadership after one purge or another. This example also suggests that you should look carefully at when the site was created. Even historians want to know if the information they are using reflects the most recent research. Consequently, many Web sites with historical information will clearly indicate—on the Web site itself—the dates of their most recent revisions or upgrades.

Although such explorations of a Web site might seem tedious, you might find a gem of information tucked away in an unexpected place. We have experienced such serendipity more than once!

And in any case, by taking this approach to exploring a Web site you can more readily begin the process of using the historian's critical method. First, ask yourself: Is what I have found *plausible*? The more fantastic the information and explanations you are offered seem to be, the more likely they will simply be fantasy. Once past that examination, consider if the Web site should be regarded as *trustworthy*. What is it about the site that inspires your trust?

Next, you will want to think about the *accuracy* of the information you have found on the Web site. Although some historical information is almost timeless, you may make a start in thinking about accuracy by your discovery of when the site was created and how recently it may have been updated. Do not despair or reject the information out of hand if you cannot readily find its most recently modified date. You can look for other indicators of accuracy. Read carefully to see if there are lots of categorical assertions. Claims of *completely, never,* or *always*—as opposed to, say, *nearly, seldom,* or *usually*—can also be indicators that the authors may not have explored all the ramifications of the topic. Also look for the qualities of impartiality and balance in the writing. Has the author taken other opinions into account?

Finally, as you would for any source, you should look for *corroboration* in other sources, not just on the Web but in reference works and other—often printed—sources. While it is not necessary to reject information that you may not be able to affirm through other sources, you will certainly need to treat it more cautiously in what you write. The story—complete with compelling photographs—of "Boilerplate," a nineteenth-century mechanical man, is a case in point. Created by comic-book artist Paul Guinan as a means of illustrating the possibilities of contemporary graphic art and storytelling, Boilerplate is *almost* believable. Certainly this source has featured in any number of high school and even college history essays. Not only doctored photographs, but also fictitious bibliographic references—mixed among real articles and links to legitimate Web sites—add to the ruse. To his credit, when the deception became public knowledge Guinan included those accounts debunking his historical "joke" among the items in the "Boilerplate News & Notes" section of his Web page.[7] But the entire effort points again to the care you must take in corroborating electronic sources you unearth in your research.

As you use all of these means to assess your research, and especially the information you find on the World Wide Web, remember that you are in essence practicing the essential evaluative skills necessary for being a historian. No matter whether your sources are primary or secondary, oral or written, found on the Web, on a CD-ROM, or in a print medium—the essence of the historian's critical method remains the same. Making a conscious effort to apply it to your electronic research work will also help you to improve the writing in your completed history essay.

REVISION

When you move from the notes taken during your research to writing a draft of your essay, the electronic environment does pose special hazards if you are not cautious. In particular, the ease of block and click operations used to capture and move electronic text from one file (or even a Web page) to another can be a temptation for including large segments of a source in your notes—and then in your essay. If you use this technique in note-taking, you will need to be certain you insert quotation marks and also mark those notes as quotations. Failing to do so could lead to careless insertion of some material you have copied directly into your essay. And even if you are simply careless and have no intent to deceive anyone, you will be guilty of plagiarism. Remember: it is *your* responsibility to avoid such errors.

---

[7] Paul Guinan, Boilerplate: The Mechanical Marvel of the Nineteenth Century, http//www.bigredhair.com/boilerplate, updated August 2003 (accessed 15 April 2006); the deception is discussed in "The Art of the Hoax," *U. S. News & World Report*, special issue, 26 August–2 September 2002.

Attending to such issues as you begin drafting your essay will also keep you focused on the possibilities for continual revision. Writers have long made revisions even on their first drafts. Manuscripts of many well known nineteenth-century authors reveal such tinkering with their work—crossing out passages, adding others, writing new text in the margins, until the manuscripts were nearly impossible to read. Then they had to start again on a fresh piece of paper! But no matter how messy, they saved the originals (as their archived papers attest) so they might go back and look again at their initial writing efforts.

Word-processing programs have, of course, made that process easier, although with one potential disadvantage. Often the original inspirations are gone, erased from the screen and replaced by a new version. We have found this to be a particular problem in our writing, and have taken to saving several versions of electronic drafts. Sometimes we open a new window on our computers and work separately on what seems to be a troublesome passage. Then we save that as a separate file so we can go back and look at it again. With the vast digital storage capacity of modern electronic devices, we can save many of these, but we are careful to give each a distinct filename. And we are grateful that our computers date and time each saved file so we are able, if necessary, to reconstruct the sequence of our thoughts. We believe the potentials of our electronic writing tools—even more than the quick availability of information on the Internet—mark perhaps the greatest contributions of our electronic age to the writing of historians.

Certainly you are familiar with the word-processing process. But in our experience, students often do not appreciate—or in any case do not fully utilize—many features of electronic writing programs to revise and improve what they write. Yet no such program, no matter how advanced or up-to-date, will be helpful until you learn how to use it effectively. Many colleges and universities have adopted particular word-processing programs as a standard for their campuses and frequently provide technical assistance in using them. Take advantage of such help! Rather than an indication of your ignorance, doing so is a signal of your intent to improve your writing. Recent editions of word-processing programs often have very useful HELP menus or utilities included. Take advantage of them as well, both to learn how the program works and to refresh your memory about features you infrequently utilize.

But it is unlikely you will need to learn all the features before you begin to write. At a minimum, though, you will want to know how to use **bold** or *italic* text, set margins, change fonts, insert special characters (such as the currency symbols £, ¥, and €), add page numbers, and, of course, insert footnotes (and endnotes). We have appreciated the ease with which our word processors allow us to change our citations from footnotes to endnotes and back again. You will too, if you first used one format and then discover your instructor would prefer another. We have found, however, that occasionally the automatic formatting of footnotes (much more so than endnotes) may result in awkward placement of references. You may need to manually alter the number of lines of text on a page to adjust the placement of the notes. If you do not immediately have someone who can assist you in mastering these functions, you may not need an expansive (and all too frequently expensive!) reference manual for the program you are using. First, ask a fellow student or your instructor, then try the program's HELP features or a campus computer help service. The time you spend will be well rewarded with an essay that looks and reads as you really want it to.

Perhaps the greatest advantage of using a computer and a word-processing program for writing is the capacity to readily make changes to the text of your essay, not only as you begin to write a draft but also when you return to make corrections after final proofreading. You can block and copy whole sections of what you have written and move them as you write and rewrite. And you can easily correct errors you have made typing or in writing your text. Frequently the newer programs will do some of this automatically, or almost automatically, for you. Take care when using such features. The programs are often designed to make such changes with minimal, if any, input from the writer. Remember: you are responsible for what you write. So be certain that any such changes reflect what *you* want to say. If you can set which items may be autocorrected, do so. If you cannot, you may wish to turn off any autocorrect functions. In any case, always read over the final text of your essay and edit it yet again yourself before you submit it to your instructor.

Similarly, the word-processing programs we use—and likely yours as well—are invaluable for checking our spelling, but only against the words stored in their memories. If you can add words to the spell-checker, by all means do so; that way terms that may be particular to your topic will not be marked as misspelled. But be careful when you enter those words, making sure the spelling you wish to use is the one you actually save. We always read what we have written on the screen and study each of the errors identified by the program; we urge you to do the same. Most often we correct those the computer has spotted. But we also know that in the binary logic of the computer some mistakes are not readily identified. For example, if you refer to a particular *sight* where you have found valuable sources for your essay, that will not be marked as misspelled, even though your instructor may wonder why you were searching for something you could see out your window rather than on a Web *site*. There are many other examples. Therefore, after re-reading our essays and making revisions on our computer screens, we have come back to the practice of also printing out a manuscript, going over it carefully with pen or pencil, and only then inserting final corrections and revisions in the computer. You may wish to consider this approach as well. But above all, you must take special care to read your work over multiple times.

Other word-processing innovations may not be as useful to you in the writing process. Among these, grammar checking functions are one of those which can be both helpful and also mystifying. When we have changed a word from singular to plural and forgotten to change the corresponding verb, the program usually marks the error, and we appreciate that. But sometimes whole phrases are noted as problematic which, on close examination, seem to be exactly as we intended and easily read. Also the thesaurus on our word processors frequently offers only limited options for potential synonyms. We still prefer a printed version, especially the new *Oxford American Writer's Thesaurus* which is particularly valuable for identifying subtle differences in word usage and meanings.[8] But our least favorite word-processing innovation is the autosummarizing option that seldom achieves anything like the "executive summary" it promises. We never use this option, preferring to make our own summaries of what we have written, and urge you to do the same.

Recent upgrades in word-processing programs may also facilitate revisions through peer-editing and similar processes. These editing functions, sometimes called "track changes" features, permit several people to read the same document file and to suggest deletions, insertions, and comments—each using distinctive colors that identify their recommendations. As the author, you may want to ask several friends to read a computer file with your essay and make electronic editorial suggestions. If they do so sequentially, each adding new advice, you can come back to your essay in a single file with a variety of comments and ideas for improving what you have written. Most such programs then allow you to accept or reject each of those changes and incorporate decisions about them into your final document. This sort of collaborative writing and revision process does take some getting used to, but has the advantage of easily consolidating comments and making it relatively easy to incorporate them into your final draft. It is a useful writing innovation that we encourage you to explore.

Finally, we again want to urge you to make back-up copies of your work at each stage in the writing process—from your initial inquiries, through your research, and also in writing both drafts and your final essay—to make back-up copies of your work. Make multiple electronic copies of your essay, and print a paper copy as well. Too often students have come to us ashen-faced, reporting they

---

[8] Christine A. Lindberg, comp., *The Oxford American Writer's Thesaurus* (New York: Oxford University Press, 2004).

have lost, erased, or destroyed the only disk on which they saved their essay. While we can and do sympathize, and grieve with them, there is seldom much we can do to help. Remember: it is up to you to prevent losing your hard work!

Without question, all the processes we discuss in this book related to writing about history have been modified and even improved with advances in electronic technologies. Use them if you can. But as you do so, carefully ask yourself questions below.

Writer's Checklist

_____ ✔ Have I used electronic technologies to assist in my writing rather than as an end in itself?

_____ ✔ Did I carefully consider the parameters of each Web search I used to find information?

_____ ✔ Have I tried using the Internet to ask questions of historians and others about my topic?

_____ ✔ Have I used online library catalogs and other electronic databases to find sources on my topic?

_____ ✔ Have I been skeptical of the electronic sources I found and applied the historian's critical method in evaluating them?

_____ ✔ Are my electronic notes and drafts saved in multiple files and kept in separate locations?

_____ ✔ Have I been very careful to identify any quotations I have taken directly from my electronic sources?

_____ ✔ Am I cautious in relying on my word processor in making editorial changes to my essay?

7

WRITING CONVENTIONS AND STYLE

■ ■ ■

Historians are a broad community, and like most communities they have their conventions, their ways of doing things. Among historians, writing conventions are perhaps most important. These are neither laws nor strict rules, and sometimes they are not logical. Rather they are simply customary. These conventions also change from age to age and differ from region to region. Still historians depend on conventions and find them necessary. Members of the community notice when the conventions are challenged. If you depart from the conventions, you run the risk of not being taken seriously. Your readers may even turn hostile toward what you write because you seem to insult them by refusing to live up to their expectations. It makes no sense for a writer to irritate readers. It's hard enough to get them to pay attention to you without putting more obstacles in their way!

At the same time, all writers express themselves in their own style, and every historian offers an individual approach to the past. Certainly style in writing varies from writer to writer, and general agreement on style is hard to come by. Some historians are vivid and dramatic; others are content to be more prosaic. Yet within the historical community substance is always to be prized over what Peter Gay describes as "a historian's emotional style" in writing about the past. "Instructive as the historian's selection of expressive techniques and unconscious coloring of narrative may be," Gay concludes that each historian's "habit of doing research and offering proof" is a better guide to a historian's "professional style." Gay acknowledges, however, that all these elements of style are "also proof of [the historian's] unconquerable subjectivity."[1]

No writer can please everybody. Shape your own style by making it as readable as you can, trying at the same time to avoid monotony of expression. Always remember that readers will bring to your work a set of expectations based upon their sense of common conventions in historical writing. A good style combines readability and variety without running ahead of the evidence supporting it. Certainly a brief chapter cannot tell you everything you need to know about style. But since beginning writers often lack confidence in their own writing, we encourage you to seek advice. For many years, American college students have benefited from the suggestions of William Strunk and E. B. White in *The Elements of Style,* now in its fourth edition.[2] We recommend their advice to you.

In addition, we want to share a few principles drawn from research on readability and the common practice of many mature writers, including numbers of historians. These are not meant to restrict your efforts to adopt a personal style of writing; rather they are guidelines based on much experience. Pay attention to them, and to the suggestions and expectations of your instructor.

SIMPLE AND DIRECT WRITING

Some of the best advice about writing is summarized in the title of a book on the subject: *Simple and Direct,* by the respected American historian, Jacques Barzun. Of course, writing well is not always that simple, even if you follow the all too common advice to "write as we speak. That is absurd," as Barzun plainly writes:

---

[1] Peter Gay, *Style in History* (New York: McGraw-Hill, 1974), 9, 197.
[2] William Struck and E. B. White, *The Elements of Style,* 4th ed. (Boston: Allyn and Bacon, 1999).

Most speaking is not plain or direct, but vague, clumsy, confused, and wordy. This last fault appears in every transcript from taped conversation, which is why we say *"reduce to writing."* What is meant by the advice to write as we speak is to write *as we might* speak if we spoke extremely well. This means that good writing should not sound stuffy, pompous, highfalutin, totally unlike ourselves, but rather, well—"simple & direct."[3]

In addition to the sensible advice that you read your essay carefully—even reading it aloud to be sure you have written what you intended—there are several key areas to keep in mind as you draft your essay. Following these conventions will help you develop a personal writing style which will serve you, and your readers, well.

Write in coherent paragraphs.

Paragraphs are groups of sentences bound together by a controlling idea and intended to help readability. Indentations break the monotony of long columns of type. They help readers follow the text with greater ease, providing special help when they lift their eyes from the page and must find their place again. Paragraphs signal a slight change in subject from what has gone before and announce that the paragraph to follow will develop a thought that can usually be summarized in a simple statement. A good rule of thumb is to have one or two indentations on every typed manuscript page. It is only a rule of thumb—not a command. And for historical writing it is also a good idea to avoid the one- or two-sentence paragraph common in journalism.

All paragraphs are built on the first sentence, and the succeeding sentences in the paragraph should run in a natural flow from it. In any good paragraph you can draw lines between connectors, sometimes a word in one sentence that is repeated in the next. The connectors tie your sentences together—and therefore link your

---

3 Jacques Barzun, *Simple and Direct: A Rhetoric for Writers* (New York: Harper and Row, 1975), 12–13.

thoughts. You can often test paragraph coherence by seeing if every sentence has connectors that join its thought in some way to the previous sentence all the way back to the first sentence in the paragraph. Other paragraphs may be more like lists of more or less interchangeable items that support the general statement made in the first sentence. Of course, all paragraphs do not fall neatly into these two categories. But in all good paragraphs and essays (or chapters of books), patterns of repetition hold all prose together. Short-term memories require this kind of repetition so that readers are continually reminded of what has gone on before. Each sentence both repeats something from previous sentences—a word, a synonym, or an idea—while adding something new to the information the readers already possess.

Look for the connectors in this paragraph from a recent article in *The American Historical Review,* in which historian Lizabeth Cohen discusses the development of shopping malls and the role of real estate developers in creating them.

> While bringing many of the best qualities of urban life to the suburbs, these new "shopping towns," as [Victor] Gruen called them, also sought to overcome the "anarchy and ugliness" characteristic of many American cities. A centrally owned and managed Garden State Plaza or Bergen Mall, it was argued, offered an alternative model to the inefficiencies, visual chaos, and provinciality of traditional downtown districts. A centralized administration made possible the perfect mix and "scientific" placement of stores, meeting customers' diverse needs and maximizing store owners' profits. Management kept control visually by standardizing all architectural and graphic design and politically by requiring all tenants to participate in the tenants' association. Common complaints of downtown shoppers were directly addressed: parking was plentiful, safety was ensured by hired security guards, delivery tunnels and loading courts kept truck traffic away from shoppers, canopied walks and air-conditioned stores made shopping comfortable year 'round, piped-in background music replaced the cacophony of the street. The preponderance of chains and franchises over local stores, required by big investors such as insurance companies, brought shoppers the latest national trends in products and merchandising techniques. B. Earl Puckett, Allied Stores' board chair, boasted that Paramus's model shopping centers

were making it "one of the first preplanned major cities in America." What made this new market structure so unique and appealing to businessmen like Puckett was that it encouraged social innovation while maximizing profit.[4]

As we have said, the paragraph is a flexible form, and these suggestions about its structure are not rigid rules. But if you think of them when you write, you will develop greater coherence to your thought, and you can develop a feel for what should be in a paragraph and what not.

Keep sentences manageable.

Your sentences, too, should always focus on the most important idea you want to make in that statement. Try not to entangle your sentences with other information you cannot readily develop or that is not related directly to some previous information in your essay. One way to keep sentences manageable is to avoid multiplying dependent clauses that act as adjectives or adverbs and modify other elements in a sentence. While they are necessary to writing, most readable writing does not use a dependent clause in every sentence. A sentence may have one or two dependent clauses. But a couple of sentences that come after it may have no dependent clauses at all—as in this paragraph from Margaret Darrow's article concerning the self-denial apparent in the writing of French battlefield nurses in World War I.

> In the end the nurses' memoirs, like the commentaries, left intact the incongruity, even the opposition, of women and war. Targets of as much criticism as praise, nurses in their memoirs absolved themselves of the charge of pursuing feminine emancipation, solidarity, and values at the expense of masculine suffering by subordinating their wartime experience to the soldier's story. Rather than script a role for the volunteer

---

[4] Lizabeth Cohen, "From Town Center to Shopping Center: The Reconfiguration of Community Marketplaces in Postwar America," *The American Historical Review*, 101 (1996): 1056.

nurse alongside the soldier in the War Myth, even the grimmest and most "realistic" of the nurses' memoirs placed the wounded soldier on a pedestal and the nurse, head bowed, at his feet, her emotional suffering a tribute to his sacrifice. In their personal accounts, France's nurse memoirists helped erase their own experiences from the public memory of the war. Their works did not reshape the War Myth to include women; instead they commemorated World War I as the trench-fighters' war and confirmed the essence of the war experience as masculinity.[5]

We are not suggesting that you should avoid dependent clauses altogether, but we are saying that you should not make them so numerous they cause you to lose control of your sentences and make your prose difficult to read. Do avoid writing in the short, choppy sentences of a first-grade reader about Dick and Jane. But you will help keep your thinking clear if in writing sentences you think first of the subject, then of what you want to say about it. Our natural way of composing sentences, whether we speak or write, is to name a subject and then to make a statement about it. Sometimes inexperienced writers are paralyzed by the thought that they begin too many sentences with the subject. They feel a laudable desire to vary their sentences by changing the beginnings and adding explanatory phrases. Yet it seldom improves your writing to bury your real subject in a dependent clause. Indeed, most readable writers use dependent clauses only once or twice in every three or four sentences. The main action of your sentence should be in the main clause. In that clause you should identify the subject and the action or activity involving your subject, which usually means keeping subjects as close to their verbs as possible.

As with most writing conventions, this is not an absolute requirement. Every writer sometimes puts a word or a phrase or even a clause between a subject and a verb. But take care not to overdo it. Here is a fine, readable paragraph by historians Oscar and

---

5 Margaret H. Darrow, "French Volunteer Nursing and the Myth of War Experience in World War I," *The American Historical Review*, 101 (1996): 106.

Lilian Handlin, from their book, *Liberty in Expansion;* note the close relation between subjects and verbs in the sentences—even in the dependent clauses.

> The healing image meant much to a government, not all of whose statesmen were pure of heart and noble of impulse. On January 30, 1798, the House of Representatives being in session in Philadelphia, Mr. Rufus Griswold of Connecticut alluded to a story that Mr. Matthew Lyon of Vermont had been forced to wear a wooden sword for cowardice in the field. Thereupon Mr. Lyon spat in Mr. Griswold's face. Sometime later, Mr. Griswold went to Macalister's store on Chestnut Street and bought the biggest hickory stick available. He proceeded to the House, where, in the presence of the whole Congress and with Mr. Speaker urging him on, he beat Mr. Lyon about the head and shoulders. An effort to censure both actors in the drama failed.[6]

Making sure that you connect the subjects of your sentences closely to the verbs which describe the actions they are taking—and that you use singular subjects with singular verbs, and plural subjects with plural verbs—will also help you focus on another important stylistic element of good writing.

Avoid the passive voice.

In sentences using the passive voice, the verb acts on the subject. In the active voice, the subject acts through the verb. Here is a sentence in the active voice:

```
President John F. Kennedy made the decision to
invade Cuba.
```

Here is a sentence in the passive voice:

```
The decision was made to invade Cuba.
```

---

6 Oscar and Lilian Handlin, *Liberty in Expansion: 1760–1850* (New York: Harper and Row, 1989), 160.

You can see at once a problem with using the passive voice. It often hides the actor in the sentence. In the active voice we know who made the decision. In the passive voice we do not know who made the decision unless we add the clumsy prepositional phrase "by President John F. Kennedy."

Announcements by governments frequently use the passive voice. "Mistakes were made," according to one government press release that we read not long ago. The passive shields us from knowing who made the mistakes. We sometimes receive essays from students who write in the passive voice, thinking that will absolve them from writing anything which suggests they have learned who did what. Of course, if that effort is successful, it also reveals that they have done the hard historical work necessary to write stories about the past that they intended to be true.

Readable historians use the passive only when they have a reason for doing so. Use the passive when the obvious importance of the sentence is that the subject is acted upon:

> Bill Clinton was elected to a second term as President of the United States in November 1996.

The passive may also help keep the focus of a paragraph on a person or group where the agent is understood throughout. In the following paragraph from a history of the Russian Revolution of 1917 and afterward, the passive is used several times. We have indicated clauses using the passive in italics. Study them to understand how the author uses the passive voice:

> The Kronstadt Naval Base, an island of sailor-militants in the Gulf of Finland just off Petrograd, *was by far the most rebellious stronghold of this Bolshevik vanguard.* The sailors were young trainees who had seen very little military activity during the war. They had spent the previous year cooped up on board their ships with their officers, who treated them with more than the usual sadistic brutality since the normal rules of naval discipline did not apply to trainees. Each ship was a tinderbox of hatred and violence. During the February Days the sailors mutinied

with awesome ferocity. *Admiral Viren, the Base Commander, was hacked to death with bayonets, and dozens of other officers were murdered, lynched or imprisoned in the island dungeons. The old naval hierarchy was completely destroyed* and effective power passed to the Kronstadt Soviet. It was an October in February. *The authority of the Provisional Government was never really established, nor was military order restored.* Kerensky, the Minister of Justice, proved utterly powerless in his repeated efforts to gain jurisdiction over the imprisoned officers, *despite rumours in the bourgeois press that they had been brutally tortured.*[7]

The focus of the paragraph is the consequence of the uprising of the sailors at Kronstadt. Thus, in this paragraph, the passive helps to keep that focus.

Our best advice is this: When you use the passive voice, ask yourself why you are doing so. If you do not have a clear reason for the passive, rewrite your sentence using the active voice.

Write about the past in the past tense.

Inexperienced writers also sometimes strive for dramatic effect by shifting their prose into the historical present. They may write something like this:

> The issue as Calvin Coolidge sees it is this: The government has been intervening too much in private affairs. He is now the head of the government. He will do as little as possible. He takes long naps in the afternoon. He keeps silent when people ask him favors. He says things like this: "The chief business of the American people is business." He does not believe the government should intervene in the business process. Within a year after Coolidge leaves office, the Great Depression begins.

---

[7] Orlando Figes, *A People's Tragedy: A History of the Russian Revolution* (New York: Viking, 1997), 394–395.

Such an effort is usually intended to provide life to the drama of history, to make it seem that it is all happening again as we read. Some students copy this form from what they hear on television, and in particular from sportscasters who have adopted similar phrasing in an attempt to make their reports more exciting. But in American as well as British historical convention, it is most appropriate to use the past tense to write about the past. The present becomes tedious after a while—and often confusing.

It is, however, permissible to use the present tense in describing a piece of writing or a work of art, because such works are assumed to be always present to the person who reads it or observes it. Therefore, you can write something like this:

```
The Fourteenth Amendment to the Constitution
gives to the citizens of the various states all the
rights guaranteed under the Federal Constitution.
```

However, you may often do better to use the past tense. This is especially true when you do not intend to give an extended summary of the work:

```
In his "Cross of Gold" speech delivered at the
Democratic National Convention in 1896, William
Jennings Bryan took the side of the impoverished
farmers who thought that inflation would help raise
the prices they received for their crops.
```

In this case, the emphasis is on Bryan rather than on the speech itself; thus the simple past tense seems more appropriate. Again, keeping the focus on what is most important in your writing is your best guide.

Keep descriptions under control.

Similarly, you should keep a clear focus on your main ideas when using descriptive modifiers and phrases. Among these are adjectives, which are modifiers and thus change the meaning of nouns somewhat. Adverbs modify verbs, adjectives, and other adverbs. Both adjectives and adverbs can sometimes weaken the concept of the words they modify. A good adjective or adverb, however, when well used in a necessary place, can brighten a sentence. Sometimes inexperienced writers will use several adverbs or adjectives in a usually vain effort to paint a fuller and richer picture for their readers. But too many of them thicken and slow down the flow of prose. Our best advice is to use both sparingly. The proportion of one adjective to every twelve or thirteen words is fairly constant among published writers in the U.S. The proportion of adverbs to other words is somewhat less. Of course, these proportions are not absolute. For some purposes you may have to use more adjectives and adverbs than normal. Be sure you need the adjectives and adverbs you use.

Sometimes there are other writing techniques which may accomplish similar goals and may, at the same time, add variety to your prose. Sometimes you may place descriptive words or phrases after the words they describe. If they could be removed and still leave an intelligible sentence, set the word or phrase off with commas, as in these examples:

> Henry David Thoreau, *one of the greatest American writers*, died of tuberculosis.
>
> William, *his brother-in-law*, was now King.

You may also use descriptive participial phrases, often to open sentences. But you must be sure they modify the subject you intend; otherwise you run the risk of making your prose incomprehensible and perhaps even ridiculous to readers. For example, consider this sentence:

> Living in a much less violent society, the idea that every man, woman, and child in the United States has a right to his or her very own assault rifle seems ridiculous to most Canadians.

Who or what lives in that less violent society? The idea? The sentence should read like this:

```
    Living in a much less violent society,
Canadians find ridiculous the idea that every man,
woman, and child in the United States has the
right to his or her very own assault rifle.
```

Metaphors and similes—which appeal to some familiar experience or perception to illustrate something less familiar—can also help you communicate with your readers without actually using descriptive words and phrases. In this passage, Civil War historian Shelby Foote writes of the danger sharpshooting snipers posed to troops in the line, even during lulls in the fighting:

> Because of them, rations and ammunition had to be lugged forward along shallow parallels that followed a roundabout zigzag course and wore a man down to feeling like some unholy cross between a pack mule and a snake.[8]

Such metaphors and similes enliven writing. But you should not carry them to excess. Used discreetly, they can be a great help in communicating your ideas.

However, take care to avoid clichés, the tired old expressions that we have heard time and again. The essence of a cliché is its predictability. When you read the beginning of the expression, you know what the end will be. You know that a bolt is always from the blue, although you seldom think that the person who speaks of the bolt from the blue is speaking of lightning striking on a clear day. You know that unpleasant facts are cold and hard and that the determining influence in a discussion is the bottom line. These are

---

[8] Shelby Foote, *The Civil War: A Narrative,* vol. 3 (New York: Random House, 1974), 297.

expressions that require no thought on the part of the writer and that inspire no thoughts in the reader.

Connect your first and last paragraphs.

As a final check on the simplicity and directness of your writing, test the coherence of your essays to see if the first and last paragraphs have some obvious relations. In most published writing—the first and last paragraphs of a book, or chapters in a book—have such coherence that you can read them without reading the intervening material and have at least a fairly good idea of what comes between. Now and then you will find a piece of writing where the first and last paragraphs do not have a clear verbal connection. But writers wishing to be sure that their work holds together can help their efforts by seeing to it that each essay ends in a paragraph that reflects some words and thoughts appearing in the first. Notice how Penny Sonnenburg's essay in Appendix A is constructed in this way.

You might also study articles in published journals to see for yourself how often this principle is observed in the professional writing of history. Turn through the pages of *The American Historical Review* to see how first and last paragraphs can mirror each other. (Looking at first and last paragraphs is also a good research technique; you may quickly see if the article includes information you may want to use in your own work.) You can also find this mirroring of first and last paragraphs in many of the essays appearing in popular journals of opinion such as the *Atlantic* or the *New Yorker*.

As you construct your own essays, try asking yourself the questions below as a means of keeping your own writing simple and direct.

Writer's Checklist

_____ ✔ Is each of my paragraphs a coherent whole?
_____ ✔ Have I kept my sentences short and manageable?
_____ ✔ Are subjects and verbs in my sentences clearly connected?

_____ ✔ Do I have clear reasons for the few times I use the passive voice?

_____ ✔ Do I write about the past in the past tense?

_____ ✔ Have I used descriptive words and phrases judiciously?

_____ ✔ Do my first and last paragraphs have some obvious relationship?

WORD FORMS AND PUNCTUATION

Written language, as we noted at the beginning of this chapter, is more formal than spoken language. Therefore, even simple and direct writing is more difficult than speaking. Sometimes in the physical labor of writing, our minds wander, and we make errors using words and punctuation. That is, we violate conventions. Most people can spot such errors by carefully reading their work aloud. You can usually trust your ear. When something does not sound right, try changing it. Having someone else read what you have written can also be invaluable, whether informally at your invitation or as part of a peer-editing process. The following are some sources of common difficulties. It is not intended as a complete summary of English grammar and you should certainly supplement our advice with that of your instructor. And by all means consult suggestions in an English language handbook or perhaps the chapters on "Grammar and Usage" and "Punctuation" in *The Chicago Manual of Style.*[9]

Form plurals and possessives of nouns accurately.

Be sure to note differences between plurals and collective nouns. For example, the singular is *peasant*, the plural is *peasants*, but the collective class in European history is called the *peasantry*.

---

[9] *The Chicago Manual of Style,* 15th ed. (Chicago: University of Chicago Press, 2003), 145–271.

We may call a man or woman who works in a factory a *proletarian,* and a group of them on an assembly line might be called by Marxists *proletarians.* But Marx called the whole class the *proletariat.* We may speak of a *noble* or an *aristocrat* when we speak of highest social ranks in some societies, and a group of such people would be called *nobles* or *aristocrats,* but the whole class is called the *nobility* or the *aristocracy.*

Take care not to use an apostrophe to form a plural. Do not write

```
The Wilsons' went to Washington.
```

The correct form is

```
The Wilsons went to Washington.
```

The plurals of dates and acronyms do not use the apostrophe. So you should write about the 1960s or the NCOs (noncommissioned officers such as sergeants) in the armed forces.

The apostrophe is used for the possessive, showing ownership or a particular relation. Some writers and editors add only an apostrophe to singular nouns ending in –s. But we believe the better practice is to form the possessive of these words as you would form others, like this:

```
Erasmus's works
Chambers's book
```

For plural nouns that end in –s, add just an apostrophe to from the possessive:

```
the Germans' plan
the neighbors' opinions
```

For plurals that do not end in –s form the possessive as you would for singular nouns:

```
women's history
children's rights
```

Distinguish spoken and written versions of common words.

The contraction *it's* stands for *it is* or, sometimes, *it has*. The possessive pronoun *its* stands for "belonging to it." Here are some examples:

```
It's almost impossible to guarantee safe
travel.
It's been hard to measure the effects on the
country.
The idea had lost its power before 1900.
```

Similarly, you should distinguish appropriately between the contraction *you're,* meaning *you are,* the possessive *your,* and the noun *yore* occasionally used to describe the past. Each of these should be used as in the following examples:

```
You're going to the picnic, aren't you?
Will you take your umbrella?
We'll have a good time, just as in days
of yore.
```

You will recognize that these distinctions are ones that your word processor's spell-checking program will not recognize, so they require you to be especially diligent in proofreading. Similar confusions abound with the words *site*—as in *Web site* or *historic site*—and *sight,* which describes what we do with out eyes; the verb *cite* can also cause confusion with these, especially since it is coming into unfortunate use as a noun in place of a *citation* you would make to document your sources.

Perhaps the most common such error we see in student essays is the accidental confusion between the plural possessive *their* and the noun or adverb *there,* specifying a particular place, and occasionally the contraction *they're* (for *they are*). Pay careful attention to these differences, as your failure to do so will often mark your essay as particularly careless.

Use objective case pronouns appropriately.

The nominative or subjective forms of pronouns include *I, we, he, she, who, they,* and *those.* The objective forms include versions such as *me, us, him, her, whom,* and *them.* The nominative is used as the subject of a sentence or a clause:

```
I read Huizinga's books.
The Prince said he was not the king's son.
```

The objective should be used for the object of a preposition:

```
It was a matter between him and me.
Between you and me, I made a mistake.
```

And the objective should be used in an indirect object:

```
The President gave her a cabinet position.
```

Objective forms should be used as the subject or an object of an infinitive verb. The infinitive is the verb form that includes the infinitive marker *to* and the dictionary form of the verb. Thus *to go, to be, to dwell,* and *to see* are all infinitives. The subject of the infinitive is a noun or pronoun that comes before the infinitive in a sentence and that does the action the infinitive expresses:

```
King Leopold wanted him to go at once to Africa.
```

In the preceding example, the person designated by the objective pronoun *him* will go to Africa. Since he will do the going the action expressed in the infinitive *to go*—the pronoun *him*—is the subject of the infinitive and is in the objective case.

Be certain pronouns refer to antecedents.

Pronouns stand for nouns that are said to be the antecedent of the pronoun. Definite pronouns, such as *he, she, it, him, her, they, them,* and *their,* stand for nouns that usually appear somewhere before them in a sentence or paragraph. Be sure to make the pronoun reference clear even if you must revise the sentence considerably. You will confuse readers if you write:

> The Czechs disdained the Slovaks because they
> were more cosmopolitan.

To whom does the pronoun *they* refer? Were the Czechs or the Slovaks more cosmopolitan? You must rewrite the sentence:

> The more cosmopolitan Czechs disdained the
> more rural Slovaks.

Use commas and semicolons appropriately.

Independent clauses—which could stand alone as sentences—can be separated from one another by commas, but only when you use linking words in addition. Without the linking words, you should use semicolons. Do not join independent clauses with commas alone. Study these appropriate examples:

> The McNary-Haugen bill would have provided
> subsidies for American farmers, but President
> Coolidge vetoed it in 1927.
> The people of the United States decided that
> they must give up Prohibition; the law brought
> about too many social disruptions.

You should, however, use commas to set off long introductory phrases:

> Even after the transcontinental railroad was
> completed in 1867, some pioneers still made the
> trip West by covered wagon.

Also use commas to separate items—whether words or phrases—
in a series:

> President Franklin D. Roosevelt moved to solve
> problems of unemployment, banking, and despair.
>
> William Jennings Bryan campaigned for the
> presidency in 1896 by traveling 18,000 miles,
> making 600 speeches, and attacking the "moneyed
> interests."

However, if the series following a colon contains internal punctuation, then the items should be separated by semicolons:.

> William Jennings Bryan campaigned for the
> presidency in 1986 while insisting on several key
> positions, which included: attacking many wealthy,
> "moneyed interests"; supporting farmers; and pro-
> moting the silver rather than the gold-standard.

Similarly, you can use commas to set off nonrestrictive words
and phrases, when you can substitute the word *and* for the comma
and still have a sensible sentence:

> Ralph Waldo Emerson was a tall, frail, and
> elegant man.

In this case you could write instead, "Ralph Waldo Emerson was a tall
and frail and elegant man." But do not use commas between adjectives
where you cannot sensibly replace the comma with *and*. You can say

> The three old maple trees stood on the hill.

But you cannot write "The three and old and maple trees stood on
the hill."

Carefully present and punctuate quotations.

When you use quotations in your essays, you should take special care in your use of punctuation, as well as lowercase and capital
letters. If the quotation is to blend into the text of your essay, change

lowercase and capital letters, as well as punctuation, so that the quotation will fit into your own sentence:

```
Kipling urged Americans "to take up the White
Man's burden."
```

You need not use brackets to indicate you have made such changes, nor should you use ellipsis marks (three dots, like this . . . ; some word processing programs may insert them automatically, without spaces, like this ...) at the beginning or end of the quotation. The quotation marks are sufficient to indicate you are beginning your quotation at that point. However, you should use ellipsis marks to indicate any words you have left out of the middle of a quotation.

Commas and periods, no matter whether they were in the original or you insert them as a part of your own sentences using quotations, should go *inside* the quotations marks. This will make what you write clearer to readers, which should be the goal for any essay you write. However, a question mark at the end of a quotation goes within the final quotation marks only if the quotation itself is a question. If you are using the quotation as part of a question which you wish to pose, then the question mark should go outside of the quotation marks. The same is true of exclamations. Semicolons and colons always go outside the final quotation marks, no matter if they were in the original quotation or not.

Any quotation longer than four or five lines in your essay should be indented five spaces and set up as a block within your text. Double-space such block quotations, and do not enclose them with quotation marks. The only quotations marks you should use with block quotations are those that appear within the original source you are quoting. Your instructor may want you to put block quotations in single-space text as your essays usually will not be for publication. Since it is difficult to edit single-spaced text, you would, however, always double-space any material intended for publication. The quotations we have used from the works of other historians in this book should serve as models of how you can use quotations from your sources in your own essays.

Maintain parallel form for a series.

English and American writers often use words or phrases in a series, but the units in the series must stand as grammatical equals. Therefore, you should *not* write sentences like this:

> Richelieu wanted three things for France—authority for the king, an end to religious strife, and he also wanted secure 'natural' frontiers.

This series begins with nouns modified by prepositional phrases, but the last element is a clause. The sentence should be rewritten something like this:

> Richelieu wanted three things for France—authority for the king, an end to religious strife, and secure "natural" frontiers.

Careful attention to common conventions in using words and punctuation is clearly important for your writing. Ask the questions below as a start toward improving your essay:

Writer's Checklist

_____ ✔ Have I formed plurals and possessives accurately?

_____ ✔ Do I distinguish between spoken and written versions of common words?

_____ ✔ Are my pronoun subjects and objects in the right form?

_____ ✔ Do my pronouns clearly refer to their antecedent nouns?

_____ ✔ Have I taken care to use commas and semicolons appropriately?

_____ ✔ Are quotations in my essay punctuated precisely?

_____ ✔ Have I kept the parallel forms in my series statements?

THE FINAL PRESENTATION

The appearance of your essay—in either an electronic or print version—tells readers many things about you as a writer. A slovenly, scarcely readable version signals a writer who cares little for the subject or for readers. As a writer you may care deeply; make sure your readers can see this from the final version you present to them. Computers make things easier for writers and readers alike, and most writers and students nowadays use computers with word-processing programs. Take advantage of the capabilities of the computer and create a clean copy of your essay.

Using your word-processing program, take special care to eliminate typographical errors, misspellings, words left out or duplicated, and other such mistakes. Also number the pages of your essay, even if it will be submitted only in an electronic version. Every word-processing program will allow you to do so; find the steps your program uses to number pages, and use them to insert page numbers into your essay. Your instructor may give you other specific directions about formatting your essay. Follow them. Lacking instructions, you usually will not go wrong if you follow the format of the model research paper in Appendix A of this book. Once you have completed these final corrections and formatting, you can save the final version of your essay—making sure to keep several copies, not all of them saved on your computer alone!

If a printed version of your essay is required, once you have saved the electronic file you can finally print a clean copy. Again, follow any instructions you have been given, but if you have none, here are some suggestions. Use a good quality 8 1/2 × 11-inch white bond paper. Double-space the essay and print it on one side of the page only. Leave margins wide enough for comments your instructor may wish to make, no less than one inch on the top, bottom, and each side. Use Times New Roman, Bookman Old Style, Courier or some other clean, easy-to-read type font and be sure the ink from the printer is dark enough to be read easily. If you must, and if your instructor will accept a handwritten essay, use lined white paper and write in dark blue or black ink on every line. Use a cover page giving your name, the name of your instructor, the name of your course, and the time your class meets. Fasten the pages of your essay with a paper clip or with a staple in the upper-left corner. Binders, however, are almost always a nuisance to the instructor, adding bulk and making it awkward to write comments in the margins. It seldom is helpful to use them.

The presentation of your essay—as an electronic file or a printed paper—is the last place where your adherence to historians' conventions is evident. But it is the first impression your instructor will have of your essay! Take advantage of that opportunity. But remember, if you ignore the conventions, you may discover that the grade you receive may be less than you desire.

DOCUMENTING SOURCES

■ ■ ■

When you write about history—or any other topic that requires research—you must use documentation that will allow readers to verify your sources. Indeed, to write history is always to write about sources. Your readers might want to check the evidence to see if you have cited it accurately and interpreted it soundly. Historians also use the documentation in books and articles they read to help them in their own research. When you use information gathered from a source, tell your readers where to find the quotation or the information. When you quote the exact words of a source, enclose those words in quotation marks or use a block quotation to let readers know they are those of another author, and make a citation to the source of the quotation. If you summarize or paraphrase a source, let readers know what you are doing. Otherwise you may be guilty of plagiarism; always remember that plagiarism is the writer's unpardonable sin. In a typical history essay of more than two or three pages, you will have many more citations to ideas and paraphrased information than you will to direct quotations.

A number of style manuals provide suggestions for forms of citations, including footnotes and endnotes. The conventional practice among historians, however, is to use *The Chicago Manual of Style,* now in its fifteenth edition.[1] Generations of students have also used

---

[1] *The Chicago Manual of Style,* 15th ed. (Chicago: University of Chicago Press, 2003).

Kate L. Turabian, *A Manual for Writers of Term Papers, Theses, and Dissertations*,[2] a conveniently sized paperback condensation of the much more comprehensive *Chicago Manual of Style*. In addition to suggestions about stylistic conventions, both provide details for note citations and bibliographies (and also for parenthetical citations and associated reference lists, frequently used and recommended to students in other disciplines). Because the format of note citations and bibliographies outlined in the *Chicago Manual* (and in Turabian's book) are the most widely used by historians, we have adopted that basic style for this brief guide to documenting your sources. Unless you receive specific instructions to the contrary, we urge you to do the same.

At the end of this chapter we have included reference charts with suggestions for both note and bibliographic citations. Of course, in this *Short Guide* we provide examples only of the most common types of sources. Turabian's manual is larger than this book, and as mentioned above, it is only an abridgment of the much larger *Chicago Manual of Style*. Both contain examples of citations for many more types of sources, and you should refer to them for additional advice. To help you locate examples of citations based on the general conventions we consider below, we have indicated (by the mark ◘) appropriate sample entries from the reference charts found at the end of this chapter. Those examples should also help you to deal fully and fairly in making citations for other sources you may use in writing your essays. The good news is that common sense and care for precision and consistency can solve a multitude of problems and allow you to guide readers faithfully through the sources you have used, no matter what those sources may be.

---

2 Kate L. Turabian, *A Manual for Writers of Term Papers, Theses, and Dissertations*, 6th ed., rev. by John Grossman and Alice Bennett (Chicago: University of Chicago Press, 1996). A new seventh edition is expected by 2007, which should reflect changes based on the fifteenth edition of the *Chicago Manual*, including consideration of electronic sources.

BASIC PRINCIPLES

Whatever citation style you are expected to use, it must lead readers to the precise location of material quoted or summarized in your essay. This requires that you pay particular attention to a number of details and make certain that they are presented carefully and consistently in your citations. Read Penny Sonnenburg's essay in Appendix A and note the forms of citations she uses. Although some of her sources are mentioned in the text, for the most part she uses footnote citations in her essay. They could just as well have been placed at the end of the paper as endnotes. Some institutions and individual teachers, as well as book and journal publishers, prefer one over the other for a variety reasons. From the writer's perspective, modern word-processing programs have simplified the formatting and placement of either footnotes or endnotes as well as the capacity to change from one to the other almost at will. If you are unsure which to use, ask your instructor. In our own experience, both as students and faculty members, most instructors simply ask students to be consistent.

There are some basic principles you should always keep in mind when choosing sources for your essay; you can also use them to help in deciding what information to include in citations of your documentation.

Authorship

The first principle to consider is authorship. Who created the work in question? Is there just one author, or are there several? Be sure to list multiple authors appropriately, especially in bibliographies (◘ *n1, n4, b3*). Occasionally, a book may have an editor who is acknowledged as the principal creator of the work. For such a source, the bibliographic entry would look very similar to that for an authored book (◘ *b1a*), while a note citation to one of the items within the book would be similar to that for any collection of essays (◘ *n8*). For a second entry by the same author or authors in a bibliography, replace the name with a dash (or underscore line) about six spaces long in place of the names; look at the Select Bibliography of Student Resources at the end of this book to see an example of how to do so.

A very few sources may have several individuals who contributed to the fundamental creation and presentation of the work. Most often these are editors and/or translators in addition to the main author (■ *n5, b8*); their names will be indicated prominently, usually on the title page of books and at the beginning (or occasionally at the end) of published articles. In recent years, some books—and especially textbooks—may have a long list of production credits on the copyright page, the page in the front matter that presents publication data, as does this book. An editor mentioned there is not credited in a citation for that source. If there is no author named for a source, or if the source is acknowledged as being anonymous, begin your citation with the title (■ *n6, b11*).

Some authorship questions can be confusing. A book review, for example, has the reviewer as the principal author of that source, although the author of the book being reviewed should also be mentioned (■ *n14*). In personal communications, such as letters or e-mails, the person writing should be listed first even though the person being written to is usually identified as well (■ *n25, n26*). Interviews are slightly more complex, as both the person being interviewed and the interviewer contribute directly to the creation of the interview. But since the person being interviewed is usually assumed to be the one supplying the crucial information (at least for historical research), their name is listed first even though the interviewer should be listed as well (■ *n23*).

Titles

The second basic element for each citation is the title. What is the source called? In the case of articles in a journal or newspaper, there will be more than a single title. The complete title of a book or pamphlet should be in italics (■ *n2, b7*). Similarly, the title of a periodical—a scholarly journal, magazine, or newspaper—should be in italics (**◘** *n9, b11*). Italics are also used for motion pictures, paintings, sculpture, and plays (**◘** *n22, b20*). But use quotation marks for short poems or speeches that have titles, just as you would for articles within a journal, magazine, newspaper, or in a collection of essays in book form (**◘** *n9, n11, b8, b12*). A few types of sources—such as interviews, letters, and manuscripts—are merely described in regular type without quotation marks (**◘** *n23, n25, b15*). The same is true of Web site titles that are not otherwise titles of books or articles (**◘** *n17*); however, an original essay within a Web site would be treated as an article and enclosed within quotation marks (**◘** *n16*).

Location

Since a major purpose for the citation is that readers may find the same work, the third important element in your citation should be the location where you found the information. For books, this means place of publication and the publisher (**◘** *n2, b4*). For scholarly journals, you will need to list the volume and sometimes the issue number (if the journal paginates each issue separately), and also the appropriate page numbers (**◘** *n9, b9*). For newspapers divided into sections, you will need to include those in your citation as well (**◘** *b12*). Often Web sites and other electronic sources of information do not divide even long items into numbered sections or use page numbers. In such cases you need to use a discrete URL which will take a reader directly to the information you have found (**◘** *n16, b16*). At other times you may also want to indicate a search term you used to locate the specific information within the particular electronic file (**◘** *n17, b17*). (We have included further advice about citations for electronic sources later in this chapter.) For manuscripts or documents in archives, you will need to indicate both the collection name and the repository where they may be found, as well as any further location identifiers used by the repository or archive (**◘** *n15, b15*).

Date

The final element to consider is the date of your source. In the case of books, it is the year of publication (◘ *n1, b2*); for journals, it is the year (and perhaps the month) of publication in addition to the volume number (◘ *n9, b9*). Newspaper and magazine citations usually include only the date, not the volume and issue numbers (◘ *n12*). For Web sites, the date the particular source was created should be included (◘ *n16, b17*); if the only date available is that of the most recent revision, that should be cited and so indicated. Many high quality, reputable Web sites have such information clearly visible on the opening page of the site; in other cases, you may need to view the source information from your web browser to determine these dates. If no such dates are available, you should indicate *n.d.* for no date. Given concerns about the impermanence of URLs (and indeed of Web sites themselves), many scholars suggest you also add the date you accessed the material on the Web, including that within parentheses (◘ *n16, b17*). This practice is not universal; in fact, the current edition of the *Chicago Manual* does not recommend it as a usual practice. We disagree and believe your instructors especially will appreciate knowing when you located the item in your research.

Shortened Forms for Subsequent Note Citations

When we first began our careers as historians, writers commonly used Latin abbreviations to make subsequent citations to sources they had already identified. This habit has gradually disappeared in academic writing. In their most recent editions, both the *Chicago Manual* and Turabian's condensed guide recommend against using most of these. Both still suggest it may be appropriate in limited cases to use ibid. (for the Latin *ibidem,* "in the same place"). However, the increasing use of word-processing programs which permit the easy movement of text—and the associated notes—from one location in an essay to another, makes even that problematic.

All too often we have found that notes transferred by the author from one location in an essay to another cannot easily be associated with their previous referents. Thus we recommend the exclusive use of shortened forms for subsequent citations, as we show on the reference chart for note citations.

Such short forms can be both easily managed by authors and easily recognized by readers. In creating shortened references, you should use the author's (or authors') surnames; you may, however, eliminate the names of translators and/or editors from subsequent references (◻ *n5*). If you use only one work from the same author(s) in your essay, then simply indicate the appropriate page (and, if necessary, volume) number in any subsequent note citation (◻ *n9, n18*). But if you use more than one source by the same author, you will also need to use a shortened title as well—of course, keeping the original order of the words. However, for titles of three or four words, you can merely eliminate any initial article (*a, an,* or *the*) and use the entire title. In these cases, too, you should also include appropriate page references (◻ *n2, n14*).

Use the reference charts at the end of this chapter as guidelines not just for the situations we have discussed but also as models for other types of sources—keeping the basic principles for documenting sources in mind. And then compare your citations as well to the Turabian or *Chicago Manual* guides if you wish to be certain you have followed the usual historical conventions and have made them clear to your readers.

ELECTRONIC SOURCES

In recent years, historians have become more concerned about the proliferation of both primary and secondary source materials available in electronic formats. In some cases these are merely digitized versions of printed (or in a few cases, handwritten) materials. In such cases, you should first make your citation to the original version, and then indicate that you found the material on the Internet or in some other electronic form (■ *n17*). Along with most historians, we would recommend that when you have a choice and may use either a printed or an electronic version of a source, you should opt for the printed version. Not least, the problems you face in documenting your source will usually be less difficult if you do so. But there are many source materials you will only be able to use in electronic formats. Therefore it is essential that you learn to make full and complete citations to such materials in your essays.

The fifteenth edition of the *Chicago Manual* for the first time makes numerous recommendations concerning citations of electronic sources. At the same time, it "anticipates a simpler and more reliable electronic source citation method . . . for assigning permanent identifiers to sources and methods for providing access to sources using those identifiers."[3] Most of the recommendations for documenting electronic sources we make in this edition of our *Short Guide* are also interim suggestions, and for the most part follow those in the current *Chicago Manual*. Where our advice differs, we have tried to be clear by explaining our own recommendations, both in this book and in a more substantial guide one of us prepared for H-Net: Humanities and Social Sciences Online.[4] We have found that many other electronic citation guides are either based on other style manuals less familiar with historical conventions or on principles which address electronic technology issues more than concerns of historical writing. One exception is that of Professor Maurice Crouse, which includes his explanations for not adhering as closely to the new *Chicago Manual* as do we.[5] Until there is more general agreement in the historical community concerning the conventions for citing electronic

---

[3] *Chicago Manual,* 646.

[4] Melvin E. Page, "A Brief Citation Guide for Internet Sources in History and the Humanities," version 3.1 (2006), http://www.h-net.org/about/citation (accessed 29 June 2006).

[5] Maurice Crouse, "Citing Electronic Information in History Papers" (7 July 2004) http://cas.memphis.edu/~mcrouse/elcite.html (accessed 27 April 2006).

sources, we urge you to check with your instructor and consistently follow either our suggestions or those of Professor Crouse.

We do recognize the Internet poses special problems for those who want to make fixed references to documents that are frequently less than permanent and subject to periodic alteration. Yet historians and humanists have for generations faced similar problems in citing sources. Private correspondence held by families of its recipients or in duplicate copies made by authors, for example, has long posed citation difficulties similar in nature to individual e-mail correspondence or, for that matter, materials on Internet Web sites as well. And disappearing sources—such as long out of print books apparently not saved in any repository, or libraries and archives destroyed by fire—have also been of concern to writers who used such materials but whose readers may not be able to locate them. Using citations that include accessed dates can, however, offer some assurance that you have looked carefully for electronic materials which may later disappear from the Internet (◘ *n16, b17*).

No method of citation can overcome these particular problems which, instead, cry out for great foresight in planning Web sites, careful explanations and links to materials that may be moved, as well as acceptance of digital object identifiers (similar to ISBN numbers) such as those favored by the University of Chicago Press. Still, citation problems for electronic materials are, for the present, quite real. While historians should be concerned about such problems and make efforts to seek solutions, as a writer you cannot solve them. So move forward, keep the basic principles of any citation we have outlined in mind, and make your citations as clear and complete as you can.

There are certain conventions in the use of the Internet that writers of history should follow. In the past, we have recommended the use of angle (or pointed) brackets, < >, to enclose either URLs or e-mail addresses; however, the use of such brackets in some, but not all, electronic programming languages does make their use in citations problematic. Therefore, we urge you to put URLs and e-mail addresses in normal type without any brackets or parentheses, keeping the punctuation as you find it (■ *n17*). Nonetheless, some word-processing programs may automatically convert these to hyperlinks on your screen, on the assumption that you are only interested in electronic versions of your essays. Often these hyperlinks are underlined and presented in a color font which may be reproduced if you merely print your file. If you are preparing printed versions of your essays, we suggest you remove the hyperlinks (■ *b17*). To do so, move your cursor onto the link using the arrow keys on your keyboard and then use word-processing EDIT functions to remove the hyperlink. Or you may click on your right mouse button to do this.

Standard Internet practice is also to put the URL on a single, separate line, if possible. But in printed citations it is often preferable for the address to continue from one line to another. When doing so, we recommend following the new *Chicago Manual* advice to end a line with any double or single slash, but that you carry any other punctuation—such as a period, comma, hyphen, underline, tilde (~), or any other similar mark—on to the next line in your printed text. Also take care, as much as possible, to set any subsequent punctuation apart from the citation since it is not part of the URL.

Even this suggestion will not solve the problem of complex URLs that are generated when you use some search utilities. Often the resulting electronic addresses are at best unmanageable in citations and occasionally may not even be useful as hyperlinks allowing readers to reach the same site. You may find that the stable URLs generated by some high-quality databases, such as JSTOR, are unwieldy for citation, even though they may be used independently to locate the items. But in the case of Project Muse, JSTOR, and similar utilities, the items in their databases come from printed sources such as scholarly journals. Thus it is best to use the original citation information from the journal, followed by a notation like this: (accessed in JSTOR).

Other search utilities, such as those designed to find information within large and extensive Web sites, present different problems. For example, using the search utility on the main H-Net Web site to locate a citation guide for electronic sources could result in finding messages in the H-Net discussion logs containing that guide. One of these messages is identified by this URL: http://h-net.msu.edu/ cgi-bin/logbrowse.pl?trx=vx&list=h-africa&month=9602&week=d& msg=sTrnwa8l9MGdmGmkVzAhGw&user=&pw=. In this case, the URL generated by the search cannot be used independently to retrieve the document and, therefore, is not even useful in making a citation. On this matter the current *Chicago Manual* does not offer clear guidance.

There is, however, a very simple solution which is comparable to a similar circumstance in using print sources. This involves use of the abbreviation s.v. (for the Latin *sub verbo,* "under the word") in making citations to standard reference works such as encyclopedias and dictionaries that are organized into individual entries usually presented in alphabetical order. Doing so in the electronic citation just mentioned would refer to the main URL of the Web site that included the search function, then indicate to the reader that the message containing the citation guide could be found by entering the words "citation guide" in that internal search utility:

```
www.h-net.org, s.v. "citation guide".
```

Note that the final period is put outside of the quotation marks since it is not a part of the search but is rather part of the punctuation of the documentation (■ *b17*).

Both the *Chicago Manual* and Turabian suggest that such citations employing "s.v." should be used only in notes, not in bibliographies. We believe that in the case of electronic sources—although NOT for printed encyclopedias and dictionaries—using such a citation format even in bibliographies offers writers an appropriate solution to one of the difficulties posed in documenting modern electronic sources (■ *n17, b17*).

One word of caution: We do NOT recommend that you make such citations to materials you find using one of the Internet-wide search engines such as Yahoo, Google, or AltaVista. Those search utilities take you to individual Web sites which you should document separately. To make your citation to the search engine itself would be comparable to citing a book by merely referring to the library catalog in which you had first found a reference to it! Only use the s.v. (or s.vv. for multiple search terms) format for electronic searches you make from the home page of a particular Web site that contains within it the material you have used in your essay, whether using that Web site's search utility or an EDIT command on your web browser to "find (on this page)."

Citations to e-mail and listerv messages also present problems, although even these have analogs in well-accepted conventions for the citation of similar sources. The person writing is clearly the author, although the person or group receiving the message should be noted as well, along with the date of the communication (■ *n26*). Many listserv messages are available in some form of publicly available electronic archive. If so, you should document that availability in your citation (■ *n24*); if there is no archive, the citation would end with the date. Precisely because so many listserv and e-mail messages are not available to most researchers in an electronic archive, some historians eschew them as sources. Yet just as historians may occasionally wish to document information received in private letters they have received, you may need to document such unarchived messages to an electronic mailing list or even private e-mails that have served as valuable sources for your essay. Some historians do insist on including the author's e-mail address as a means of verifying the information, although you should never do so without permission.

Despite the problems we have mentioned, we remain confident solutions to any documentation problems for source material on the Internet and in other electronic formats are possible. It is not necessary—and in fact inappropriate—simply to avoid such sources for lack of standard conventions for making citations to them. Should you confront such problems, ask your instructor or a reference librarian how you might deal with them. And use the citation reference charts at the end of this chapter as guides in making decisions about how to document all the sources you have consulted in writing your essay. If you still have questions, you may write to Melvin Page at pagem@etsu.edu and pose the problem; he will try to offer our best suggestions for a solution.

NOTES AND BIBLIOGRAPHIES

When writing history essays, the conventional forms for citing sources have long been notes and bibliographies. While both present essentially the same information in similar ways, they do serve different functions. Notes are written in the same manner, whether they are presented as footnotes—at the bottom of each page where the citation occurs—or as endnotes—at the end of the essay, before the bibliography. Of course, each note should be preceded by a number referring to the place in your essay where you want to document sources for what you have written. These numbers, both in the text and at the start of each note, are best set as superscript numerals (◘ *n1*), something easily achieved in a word-processing program. A style for presenting citation information in notes has evolved over the years, and that presented here and in the *Chicago Manual* has become the conventional standard for historians. Each note should begin with a paragraph indent so it can easily be distinguished in your text.

This style and format for writing notes is intended for quick, easy reading, especially at the bottom of a page of text but also in quick glances at a list positioned at the end of the essay or book. Readers want to know why your story is intended to be true. To convince them, you need to make clear what evidence you used in supporting your statements and connect that information directly to what you write. Historians use notes to do this, and you should as well. Notes also help readers search for the same specific bits of information they read about, should they wish to do so. You should take similar advantage of the notes you find in your sources when preparing to write your own essays.

Bibliographies, on the other hand, are more formal. While these citations are composed of much the same information as notes, they are alphabetized by the last name of the author, and the punctuation is somewhat different. For a second work by the same author(s), use a six space line to replace the name(s); the Select Bibliography of Student Resources at the end of this book provides an example of how to do this. If there is no author, bibliographic citations begin with the title, which is used for alphabetizing such entries along with others (◘ *b6, b11*). In *Chicago Manual* style, a bibliographic entry does not use parentheses for publishing information; each component of the entry is separated by periods. Entries for articles, and other sources included within printed books or journals have inclusive page numbers (◘ *b8, b9*). Dates for journals are, however, placed in parentheses to better distinguish them, although this is not done for newspapers and magazines (◘ *b9, b12*). And each bibliographic entry is set apart using a "hanging indent" system easily created with a word-processing program.

Bibliographies are placed at the end of an essay or book to allow readers to see quickly what works have been cited or consulted by the author. A bibliography shows whether the writer has searched a wide variety of sources and whether he or she knows the latest literature in a field of inquiry. But some individual items are not generally included in a bibliography even though you may have cited them in note citations (◘ *n21–n26*). If you have questions, be sure to consult with your instructor about what you should include in your bibliography. You may sometimes be asked to make your research efforts clearer by presenting an annotated bibliography, which includes a brief comment on the contents of the book, article, or other source. If you are asked to annotate your bibliography, begin your comments on a separate line, indenting the first line of your annotation text. The Short Bibliography of Student Resources at the end of this book is a model for your own annotated bibliography.

Use the following citation reference charts to aid you in writing the bibliographic and note citations that will document your history essays.

Note *Citations Reference Chart*

Item ◘	Type of Source	Note Citations	Subsequent Citations
n1	book (one author)	[1] Jerry H. Bentley, *Old World Encounters* (New York and Oxford: Oxford University Press, 1963), 183.	[2] Bentley, 185.
n2	book (subsequent edition)	[1] John Thornton, *Africa and Africans in the Making of the Atlantic World, 1400–1800,* 2d ed. Studies in Comparative World History (Cambridge and New York: Cambridge University Press, 1998), 157.	[2] Thornton, *Africa and Africans,* 159.
n3	book (two authors)	[1] Stanley L. Engerman and Robert W. Fogel, *Time on the Cross: The Economics of American Negro Slavery* (New York: W. W. Norton, 1989), 206.	[2] Engerman and Fogel, 208.
n4	book (multiple authors)	[1] Bakili Muluzi et al., *Democracy with a Price: The History of Malawi Since 1900* (Blantyre, Malawi: Jhango Heinemann, 1999), 17.	[2] Muluzi, 19.
n5	book (edited or translated)	[1] Martin Luther, *Lectures on Romans,* ed. and trans. Wilhelm Pauck (Philadelphia: Westminster Press, 1961), 101.	[2] Luther, 76.
n6	book (author/editor unnamed)	[1] *Cultures and Time* (Paris: Unesco Press, 1976), 7.	[2] *Cultures and Time, 9.*
n7	book in a series	[1] Robert C. Post, *Technology, Transport, and Travel in American History,* Historical Perspectives on Technology, Society, and Culture (Washington, DC: American Historical Association, 2003), 53.	[2] Post, 54.
n8	article in collection of essays	[1] Gabrielle Spiegel, "History and post-modernism," in *The Postmodern History Reader,* ed. Keith Jenkins (London and New York: Routledge, 1997), 261.	[2] Spiegel, 263.

(Continued)

Note Citations Reference Chart

Item ◘	Type of Source	Note Citations	Subsequent Citations
n9	article in scholarly journal	[1] Denise S. Spooner, "A New Perspective on the Dream: Midwestern Images of Southern California in the Post–World War II Decades," *California History*, 76, no. 1 (Spring 1997): 48.	[2] Spooner, 49.
n10	article in popular magazine	[1] Pritt J. Vesilind, "Lost Gold: Bounty from a Civil War Ship," *National Geographic*, September 2004, 114.	[2] Vesilind, 125.
n11	article in magazine (author/editor unnamed)	[1] "War Letters," *National Geographic*, November 2005, 92.	[2] "Letters," 89.
n12	article in newspaper	[1] David E. Sanger, "Clinton Warns Japan: Fire Up Economy to Stem a Decline," *New York Times*, 4 April 1998, A1.	[2] Sanger, A2.
n13	article in reference work	[1] *Dictionary of the History of Ideas*, s.v. "Historiography," by Herbert Butterfield, 465.	[2] Butterfield, 465.
n14	book review	[1] John Thornton, review of *Landlords and Strangers: Ecology, Society, and Trade in Western Africa, 1000–1630*, by George E. Brooks, *Journal of World History* 6 (1995): 133.	[2] Thornton, review of Brooks, 133.
n15	archives document	[1] Benjamin Bowman, manuscript letter to Joseph Bowman, 24 July 1860, Bowman Family Collection, Acc. No. 23, Archives of Appalachia, East Tennessee State University, Johnson City, TN.	[2] B. Bowman to J. Bowman, 24 Jul 1860.
n16	Web site (discrete URL)	[1] Joseph C. Miller, "History and Africa/Africa and History" (8 January 1999) http://www.ecu.edu/African/sersas/jmahapa.htm (accessed 23 November 2003).	[2] Miller.

Note Citations Reference Chart

Item ◘	Type of Source	Note Citations	Subsequent Citations
n17	Web site (accessed by internal search)	[1] Irwin H. Hoover, memoir, 4 March 1913, in Library of Congress: American Memory, http://memory.loc .gov/index.html s.v. "Irwin H. Hoover" (accessed 27 April 2005).	[2] Hoover.
n18	unpublished thesis or dissertation	[1] William H. Gilbert, "From Condem-nation to Conformity: Carter and Reagan's Foreign Policy Towards the Argentine Junta, 1977–1982" (M.A. thesis, East Tennessee State University, 2005), 51.	[2] Gilbert, 53.
n19	unpublished paper	[1] Gavriel D. Rosenfeld, "Alternate History and Memory" (paper presented at annual meeting of American Historical Association, Philadelphia, 6 January 2006).	[2] Rosenfeld.
n20	motion picture (video/DVD)	[1] *Breaker Morant*, videocassette, directed by Bruce Beresford (1979; Burbank, CA: RCA/Columbia Pictures Home Video, 1985).	[2] *Breaker Morant*, 1985.
n21	photograph	[1] "An excellent example of a pack or artillery mule," photograph, in *Shavetails and Bell Sharpes: The History of the U. S. Army Mule*, by Emmett M. Essin (Lincoln: University of Nebraska Press, 1997), facing p. 85.	[2] Photograph in Essin, p. 85.
n22	work of art	[1] Jan van Eyck, *Giovanni Arnolfini and His Bride*, painting, as reproduced in Dennis Sherman et al., *World Civilizations: Sources, Images, and Interpretations*, 3d ed. (New York: McGraw-Hill, 2002), 1: 231.	[2] van Eyck, *Giovanni Arnolfini and His Bride*.
n23	interview	[1] Stambuli Likuleka, interview by Melvin E. Page, 17 August 1972.	[2] Likuleka interview.

(Continued)

Note Citations Reference Chart

Item ◘	Type of Source	Note Citations	Subsequent Citations
n24	**message in Internet discussion list**	[1] Richard Lobban, "REPLY: African Muslim Slaves in America," message to H-Africa, h-africa@msu.edu, 4 August 1995, archived at http://h-net.msu.edu/~africa/archives/august95.	[2] Lobban.
n25	**private letter**	[1] George Shepperson, letter to author, 4 October 2004.	[2] Shepperson to author.
n26	**private e-mail message**	[1] Carol Jones, e-mail message to author, 23 April 2001.	[2] Jones to author.

Bibliographic Citations Reference *Chart*

Item ◘	Type of Source	Bibliographic Citations
b1	book (one author)	Bentley, Jerry H. *Old World Encounters.* New York and Oxford: Oxford University Press, 1963.
b1a	book (editor as author)	Hilliard, Constance B., ed. *Intellectual Traditions of Pre-Colonial Africa.* Boston: McGraw-Hill, 1998.
b2	book (subsequent edition)	Thornton, John. *Africa and Africans in the Making of the Atlantic World, 1400–1800,* 2d ed. Studies in Comparative World History. Cambridge and New York: Cambridge University Press, 1998.
b3	book (two authors)	Engerman, Stanley L., and Robert W. Fogel. *Time on the Cross: The Economics of American Negro Slavery.* New York: Norton, 1989.
b4	book (multiple authors)	Muzuli, Bakili, Yusuf M. Juwayeyi, Mercy Makhambera, and Desmond D. Phiri. *Democracy with a Price: The History of Malawi Since 1900.* Blantyre, Malawi: Jhango Heinemann, 1999.
b5	book (edited or translated)	Luther, Martin. *Lectures on Romans.* Edited and translated by Wilhelm Pauck. Philadelphia: Westminster Press, 1961.
b6	book (author/ editor unnamed)	*Cultures and Time.* Paris: Unesco Press, 1976.
b7	book in a series	Post, Robert C. *Technology, Transport, and Travel in American History.* Historical Perspectives on Technology, Society, and Culture. Washington, DC: American Historical Association, 2003.
b8	article in collection of essays	Spiegel, Gabrielle. "History and Postmodernism." In *The Postmodern History Reader,* ed. Keith Jenkins, 260–273. London and New York: Routledge, 1997.
b9	article in scholarly journal	Spooner, Denise S. "A New Perspective on the Dream: Midwestern Images of Southern California in the Post–World War II Decades." *California History* 76, no. 1 (Spring 1997):45–57.
b10	article in popular magazine	Vesilind, Pritt. J. "Lost Gold: Bounty from a Civil War Ship." *National Geographic,* September 2004, 108–127.

(Continued)

Bibliographic Citations Reference Chart

Item ■	Type of Source	Bibliographic Citations
b11	article (author/editor unnamed)	"War Letters," *National Geographic,* November 2005, 78–95.
b12	article in newspaper	Sanger, David E. "Clinton Warns Japan: Fire Up Economy to Stem a Decline." *New York Times,* 4 April 1998, A1.
b13	reference work	Wiener, Philip P., ed. *Dictionary of the History of Ideas.* 5 vols. New York: Scribner's, 1973.
b14	book review	Thornton, John. Review of *Landlords and Strangers: Ecology, Society, and Trade in Western Africa, 1000–1630,* by George E. Brooks. *Journal of World History* 6 (1995): 132–135.
b15	archive collection	Bowman Family Collection. Accession No. 23, Archives of Appalachia, East Tennessee State University. Johnson City, TN.
b16	Web site (discrete URL)	Miller, Joseph C. "History and Africa/Africa and History." 8 January 1999. http://www.ecu.edu/African/sersas/jmahapa.htm. (Accessed 23 November 2003).
b17	Web site (accessed by internal search)	Hoover, Irwin H. Memoir. 4 March 1913. In Library of Congress: American Memory, http://memory.loc.gov/index.html s.v. "Irwin H. Hoover". (Accessed 27 April 2005).
b18	unpublished thesis or dissertation	Gilbert, William H. "From Condemnation to Conformity: Carter and Reagan's Foreign Policy Towards the Argentine Junta, 1977–1982." M.A. thesis, East Tennessee State University, 2005.
b19	unpublished paper	Rosenfeld, Gavriel D. "Alternate History and Memory." Paper presented at annual meeting of American Historical Association, Philadelphia, 6 January 2006.
b20	motion picture (video/DVD)	*Breaker Morant.* Videocassette. Directed by Bruce Beresford. 1979. Burbank, CA: RCA/Columbia Pictures Home Video, 1985.

APPENDIX A

■ ■ ■

Sample Student Research Paper

On the following pages you will find a sample research paper written for a course in world history using the process we have outlined in this book (and sometimes illustrating it with Ms. Sonnenburg's research experiences). Study the paper. Then consider the questions about the paper at the end. Ask smiliar questions about any essay you write for a history course.

Pay close attention to the format of the paper. Note the title page (which includes the title of the paper, the name of the author, the date the paper is turned in, the name of the course, the time of the class, and the name of the professor) as well as the footnotes and the bibliography. The margins should be set at no less than one inch on all four sides of the page. *Always* number pages, but remember that the title page is not numbered, although it is considered page one in the text of your paper.

Manifest Destiny: A Characteristic of Nations

BY PENNY M. SONNENBURG
East Tennessee State University
March 20, 2005
History 4957: Colonialism and Imperialism
Professor Melvin Page
M 2:00—4:50 pm

More than a century before John L. O'Sullivan wrote the words reflective of the expansionist fervor that gripped the United States, of "our manifest destiny to overspread the continent,"[1] the essence of the idea was already a part of what would become our national heritage. Yet as late as the 1920s, Julius Pratt proclaimed confidently in the *American Historical Review* that O'Sullivan invented the phrase.[2] Now, over a century and a half after O'Sullivan penned those well-known words, it should be apparent that the United States was not alone in its fervor and O'Sullivan merely gave dramatic voice to what was a well-developed national disposition with deep roots in the Western tradition.

In *The Power of Ideals in American History,* Ephraim Adams construed the concept of "manifest destiny" as inherent in the nature of nearly all countries, dispelling the notion that it was a unique American characteristic. Adams elaborated that the "sense of destiny is an attribute of all nations and all peoples." He claimed that if we penetrated beyond recorded history, distinct emotions of various tribes and races would provide an early understanding of "manifest destiny." Probably we would find that these tribes and races also felt themselves a "chosen people" set apart for some high purpose.[3]

---

[1] John L. O'Sullivan, "Annexation," *Democratic Review,* 17 (July and August 1845), in *Manifest Destiny and the Imperialism Question,* ed. Charles L. Sanford (New York: Wiley, 1974), 28.

[2] Julius W. Pratt, "The Origin of 'Manifest Destiny,'" *The American Historical Review,* 32(1927): 798.

[3] Ephraim Douglas Adams, *The Power of Ideals in American History* (New York: AMS Press, 1969), 67.

Adams also implied that any great nation had a belief in its destiny; larger nations wanting a place in the sun while smaller, contented nations were constantly on alert to avoid absorption by their more powerful neighbors. As historians, we can analyze and thereby illustrate that the concept of manifest destiny occurred long before 1845 and was not limited to the American people. The United States, beginning with its colonial past, utilized the essence of the concept, placing it on a higher philosophical plane. The nationalistic expansionist movement in the United States was based upon a moral ideology and appeared as an inherent quality justifying itself as a natural right.[4]

Natural right formed the historical foundation that was later used as an explanation and underlying ideology surrounding the manifest destiny movement. Natural right was basically defined as any right that "Nature," recognized in a "divinely supported system of 'natural law' inclusive of moral truths, bestows prior to or independently of political society." The beginnings of this idea can be traced back to Greek philosophers who wrote of "things that are right by nature, that is, inherently, and can be recognized by every rational being to be so."[5] Later stoic philosophers, and indeed basic Roman legal beliefs, followed the same reasoning that natural rights were among the truths contained in natural law. Sir Ernest Barker, in *Traditions of Civility,* addressed the natural law idea as a movement among the Stoic thinkers of the Hellenistic age. The large and somewhat general expression "became a tradition of human civility which runs continuously from

---

[4] Albert K. Weinberg, *Manifest Destiny: A Study of Nationalist Expansionism in American History* (New York: Johns Hopkins University Press, 1958), 12.

[5] Weinberg, 13–14.

the Stoic teachers of the Porch to the American Revolution of 1776 and the French Revolution of 1789."6 For many centuries this was directly considered part and parcel of church theology, later adopted by the Catholic Church and forming a core element of church doctrine for teachers and early canonists. This logic formed a rational basis for the physical and moral universe, hence the "theory of Natural Law had become in the sixteenth century, and continued to remain during the seventeenth and the eighteenth, an independent and rationalist system professed and expounded by the philosophers of the secular school of natural law."7 Later Christianity "harmonized these ideas of paganism with its own theology by regarding natural law as the expression of the eternal reason of God." And thus natural right came to embrace two principles in the Western tradition—secular and sacred—and set the stage for the "momentous pretension later to be called nationalism." This powerful affirmation enhanced an emerging idea that nationalities were the most likely agencies for promotion not only of the rights of particular groups, but also of the rights of mankind as a whole.8 This tendency toward an assertion of group entitlement confirmed for Adams his view of early tribes and races employing concepts of higher purpose, foreshadowing early nationalistic leanings.

Based on this *a priori* condition, there is firm ground for asserting the close relationships between the ideas usually described as nationalism, expansionism, ethnicity, natural law, and manifest

---

6 Ernest Barker, *Traditions of Civility* (Cambridge: Cambridge University Press, 1948), 312.

7 Barker, 216.

8 Weinberg, 13–14.

destiny. The rhetoric of politics, religion, and philosophy throughout early European history established a touchstone for these relationships. And early historians of Europe were instrumental in drawing attention to the connections. Tacitus, Roman historian of the Germanic peoples, described in his *Germania* such characteristics among the people about whom he wrote. "The tribes of Germany," he declared, "are free from all taint of intermarriages with foreign nations, and . . . they appear as a distinct, unmixed race, like none but themselves."9 Such tendencies were passed on to the early populations of Great Britain who were descendants of Germanic tribes. William Camden confirms this in his *Remaines concerning Britaine*, writing that "he saw God's hand in the guiding of the Angles and Saxons to England."10 This version of the "chosen people" doctrine became an early cornerstone of popular ideology in England as the New Anglican church under Elizabeth adopted the essence of its message.

Archbishop Matthew Parker, a major defender of Anglo-Saxon literature and scholarship, along with his secretary, John Joscelyn, began an inquiry of pre-Norman English history. The purpose of their study was an effort not only to prove the ancientness of new English church customs but also to promote an interest in general English history during the Anglo-Saxon period. Archbishop Parker's contemporary John Foxe, particularly emphasized

---

9 Tacitus, *The Agricola and Germania,* trans. A. J. Church and W. J. Brodribb (London: Macmillan, 1877), in Medieval Source Book, ed. Paul Halsall, http://www.fordham.edu/halsall/source/tacitus1.html, January 1996 (accessed 17 February 2005).

10 Quoted in Reginald Horsman, *Race and Manifest Destiny* (Cambridge: Harvard University Press, 1981), 12.

in his 1563 *Acts and Monuments* the "uniqueness of
the English and their nature as 'a chosen people,'
with a church lineage stretching back to Joseph
of Arimathea and his supposed visit to England,
and with John Wyclif as the true originator
of the Reformation."[11] Following the English
Revolution, and especially after the Restoration
of the monarchy, "the idea of the English nation
as the crusading agent of God's will faded" into a
minor theme in English thought. But the historical
roots of the philosophy ran deep and were
planted especially on the frontiers of English
expansionism. It is no wonder then, that "Americans
never lost the belief that they were a special,
chosen people, a people destined to change the
world for the better."[12]

The ascendancy of the English view of the
Anglo-Saxons appeared as an inherent characteristic
in the American colonies. The post-Reformation
Continental writers reinforced the myth produced by
two centuries of political and religious conflict.
"As colonial Englishmen the settlers in America
fully absorbed the mythical view of the English
past developed between 1530 and 1730."[13] Colonial
settlers did not limit their absorption to one
viewpoint. They also embraced and were inspired
by an emerging philosophy of nationalism. In an
effort to systematize nationalism, eighteenth-
century European philosophers provided the spark
for revolutionary movements of the period. The
diversity of thought found in the "culturally
nationalistic Herder, the democratic Rousseau,
the Tory Bolingbroke, and the liberal physiocrats"
was transplanted into the natural rights domain of
the American colonial psyche. These philosophers'

---

[11] Horsman, 10.
[12] Horsman, 82.
[13] Horsman, 15.

proto-nationalist doctrines basically included one—and usually both—of two basic foundations of natural right ideas. The first principle addressed the "natural rights of groups to determine upon and organize the desired form of government." The second principle declared that nations were the "natural agencies" for advancing not only the rights of particular groups but also, the rights of all mankind.[14] One does not have to have an overactive imagination to recognize this characteristic in colonial America.

In *Manifest Destiny and Mission in American History: A Reinterpretation*, historian Frederick Merk links nationalism with expansionism. He asserts that expansionism was usually associated with ideology. Merk's validation of this point leads one past the early writings of natural right into an ideological framework for expansionism. His broad, global sweeps through expansionist ideology are summarized as he concludes of the causes: "in the case of Arab expansionism it was Islam; in Spanish expansionism, Catholicism; in Napoleonic expansionism, revolutionary liberalism; in Russian and Chinese expansionism, Marxian communism." In the United States an equivalent of these ideologies appeared as manifest destiny, and the main ingredients consisted of republicanism, democracy, freedom of religion, and Anglo-Saxonism.[15] The intellectual ship that carried the settlers across the wide Atlantic also altered, and then adopted the "idea of natural right as the moral rationale of America's expansionism." In the early developmental period, the newly arrived Americans tended to stress the rights rather than the duties

---

[14] Weinberg, 13–14.

[15] Frederick Merk, *Manifest Destiny and Mission in American History: A Reinterpretation* (New York: Knopf, 1963), vii–ix.

of natural law. "The conception of natural right was first used by New England clergymen in behalf of right of ecclesiastical independency." In 1760 the concept escaped from the pulpits into the public discussion arena as Americans became concerned with their own political rights under English rule. This ideological transformation reached an initial climax with inclusion of the "inalienable natural rights with which their Creator had endowed them [Americans]" in the Declaration of Independence confirming the United States' belief in its "chosenness." Americans assumed the position "among the powers of the earth, the separate and equal station to which the Laws of Nature and Nature's God entitle them." Assuming the position of natural rights guardian, Americans justified the "right of revolution when governments became destructive of natural rights."[16]

The end of the American Revolution empowered the new nation and set it along a course that engaged the country in the manifest destiny phenomenon. This total embrace of a powerful movement allowed the misnomer that manifest destiny was a unique American feature. Early American history is laced with examples of the doctrine that have been used throughout as situational justification of the means to the end. In 1801 Jefferson's application of diplomatic and military pressure induced Napoleon to negotiate with the United States for the sale of New Orleans and a slice of coastal territory to the east. Much to Jefferson's surprise, in 1803 Napoleon sold all of the immense Louisiana territory to the United States. This enabled Jefferson to realize his main objective: possession of New Orleans and ultimate control of the mouth of the Mississippi, thus providing the much-needed outlet to world markets

---

[16] Weinberg, 16.

for the interior of the new nation.[17] Acquisition of the Louisiana Purchase also perpetuated the expansionist movement of the United States.

This expansionism continued as a nationally heartfelt but nameless movement. As early as 1818 Andrew Jackson applied his own understanding of President Monroe's instructions and led military forces into Spanish-held Florida, destroying the Indians in his path; he set into motion the natural rights claim of Americans to possession of any land that they wanted.[18] Further use of the still unnamed principle appeared as an American assumption that its destiny was that of a world power. In 1822 the Monroe Doctrine—warning the whole of Europe to stay out of the Western Hemisphere—illustrated James Monroe's belief in this idea. Monroe was certainly not alone in this belief, although there was a small vocal opposition which made the still unnamed doctrine a disputed philosophy.

The opposition movement exposed a different side to Americans as being the "chosen people." In an 1837 letter to Henry Clay, William E. Channing—the social activist and leading figure in the American Unitarian movement—wrote that "we are a restless people, prone to encroachment, impatient of the ordinary laws of progress." Channing feared the strength that the country felt at extending its boundaries—by natural right—from shore to shore was fraught with dire consequences. "We boast of our rapid growth," he continued in his letter to Clay, "forgetting that, throughout nature, noble growths are slow. . . . Already endangered by our greatness, we cannot advance without imminent peril to our institutions, union, prosperity, virtue, and

---

[17] David Goldfield et al., *The American Journey: A History of the United States* (Upper Saddle River, NJ: Prentice Hall, 1998), 261.
[18] Goldfield et al., 277.

peace. . . . There is no fate to justify rapacious nations, any more than to justify gamblers and robbers, in plunder."[19] Opposition, however, seems to have emboldened the proponents of the doctrine, which was only then surfacing in open expression.

What seemed to be the opinion of a majority of the American people at the time was featured not only in John O'Sullivan's 1845 editorial in the *Democratic Review,* but also in another article published in the same journal that year. This also addressed the Texas annexation issue and justified the addition of the new state. "Texas has been absorbed into the Union in the inevitable fulfillment of the general law which is rolling our population westward." O'Sullivan contended that Texas "was disintegrated from Mexico in the natural course of events, by a process perfectly legitimate on its Union was not only inevitable, but the most natural, right and proper thing in the world."[20] It is not ironic that the article appeared in this particular *Review*, as it was the same journal that finally gave a name—hence a formal justification—for what was believed the right of Americans: our Manifest Destiny.

Precursors to American predominance had been played out, and history was set to be made, all in the name of Manifest Destiny. This is a classic example of how, when doctrines gain names, they in turn gain legitimacy and ultimately power. The combination of the idealistic vision of social perfection through God and the pride of American nationalism in the mid-nineteenth century filled

---

[19] Quoted in Michael T. Lubragge, "Manifest Destiny: The Philosophy That Created a Nation," in From Revolution to Reconstruction, http://odur.let .rug.nl/~usa/E/manifest/manif1.htm, updated 6 March 2005 (accessed March 12, 2006).

[20] Quoted in Lubragge, "Manifest Destiny."

an American ideological need for domination of the hemisphere from pole to pole, as Monroe had implied. This was ultimately based on the concept of Americans possessing a divine providence. The strong belief of God's will for American expansion over the whole of the continent and to ultimately control the country led to a guiding call to human destiny. "It was white man's burden to conquer and christianize the land," as Kipling envisioned at the end of nineteenth century. This expanded the Puritan notion of a "city on a hill" and was secularized into Manifest Destiny, albeit a materialistic, religious, and utopian destiny.[21]

This eventually led to the fear that foreigners crossing the national frontier borders might hamper the security of the United States. The most reasonable answer was to conquer land beyond those borders and expand to other areas. This became evident when Albert T. Beveridge arose in the United States Senate and espoused the view—with utmost certainty—that "Anglo-Saxon [America] was destined to rule the world" and went on to state that "He [God] has made us the master organizers of the world to establish system where chaos reigns."[22] In speaking so boldly, Beveridge introduced an international dimension to American Manifest Destiny that justified the 1867 purchase of Alaska from Russia for $7,200,000. The price of being a world empire had risen from its earlier purchase of Louisiana from Napoleon! Indeed, not only the price, but the arrogance of this doctrine was on the rise as the expansionist fervor grew following the Spanish-American War. Congress went so far as to call for annexation of all Spanish territories. Newspapers of the time were more extreme in suggesting the annexation of Spain itself.

———————————

21 Lubragge, "Manifest Destiny."
22 Quoted in Lubragge, "Manifest Destiny."

Aspirations of an American empire were echoed in the views of other expansionists, including Theodore Roosevelt, former President Harrison, and Captain Alfred T. Mahan. Indeed the latter's treatise on the importance of naval power in international affairs was especially influential. Such voices fed what seemed to be an insatiable desire once again, manifesting itself in 1898 when America decided that it wanted control of Hawaii and took it—oddly not quite so differently as when Andrew Jackson took Florida nearly a century before. The supposed American mission to the islands came to fruition in 1959 when the United States made Hawaii its fiftieth state.[23]

Throughout American history the dual visions of the American people—of a divine providence destined by God to direct national expansion, or of a natural right to extend liberty (our own version, of course) to other parts of world—seemed to complement each other. Once again, it appeared that the means ultimately justified the end. As a people we embraced an unnamed, but not unknown, doctrine and made it our own. And, as in our previous history, we have taken concepts, ideologies, and policies—altering them to fit our own needs—and then applying them to our own country.

While this process is not totally detrimental, it hinders our ability to understand and examine American history as a part of world, as well as our own national, history. When faced with attempting to understand the philosophy of destiny and the concept of being a "chosen people," it is most beneficial to widen our lens and focus on a broader picture. When this occurs, we can then understand that the United States did not create a new doctrine but simply embellished upon principles that can be traced back to earlier "chosen people"

---

[23] Lubragge, "Manifest Destiny."

and their own individual views of natural right and
nationalism. This philosophy began as far back—if
not farther—as the Greek philosophy of Stoicism.
Viewed that way, manifest destiny is a necessary
requirement for all societies seeking a higher
purpose for their own nation and peoples. This
is not totally inconceivable since "all nations
that are worth anything, always have had, and
always will have, some ideal of national destiny,
and without it, would soon disappear, and would
deserve their fate."[24]

Bibliography

Adams, Ephraim Douglass. *The Power of Ideals in
American History*. New York: AMS Press, 1969.

Barker, Ernest. *Traditions of Civility*. Cambridge:
Cambridge University Press, 1948.

Haynes, Sam W. "Manifest Destiny." In The U.S. Mexican
War (1846-1848). http://www.pbs/org/kera//
usmexicanwar/dialogues/prelude/manifest/d2heng.html.
(Updated 6 August 1999; accessed 2 February 2005).

Horsman, Reginald. *Race and Manifest Destiny*.
Cambridge: Harvard University Press, 1981.

LaFeber, Walter. "The World and the United States."
American Historical Review 100(October 1995):
1015-1033.

Long, A. A., ed. *Problems in Stoicism*. London: Athlone
Press, 1971.

Lubragge, Michael T. "Manifest Destiny: The Philosophy
That Created a Nation." In From Revolution to
Reconstruction. http://odur.let.rug.nl/~usa/E/
manifest/manif1.htm. (Updated 6 March 2003;
accessed 30 April 2006).

---

[24] Adams, 68.

Merk, Frederick. *Manifest Destiny and Mission in American History: A Reinterpretation.* New York: Knopf, 1963.

O'Sullivan, John L. "Annexation." *Democratic Review* 17(July and August 1845). In *Manifest Destiny and the Imperialism Question*, ed. Charles L. Sanford, 26–34. New York: Wiley, 1974.

Pratt, Julius W. "The Origin of 'Manifest Destiny.'" *The American Historical Review* 32(1927): 798.

Sanford, Charles L., ed. *Manifest Destiny and the Imperialism Question.* New York: Wiley, 1974.

Tacitus, Publius Cornelius. *The Agricola and Germania*, trans. A. J. Church and W. J. Brodribb. London: Macmillan, 1877. In Medieval Source Book, ed. Paul Halsall. http://www.fordham.edu/halsall/source/tacitus1.html. (January 1996; accessed 30 April 2006).

Webb, Walter Prescott. "The Frontier and the 400 Year Boom." In *The Turner Thesis Concerning the Role of the Frontier in American History*, ed. George Rogers Clark, 87–95. Boston: Heath, 1956.

Weinberg, Albert K. *Manifest Destiny: A Study of Nationalist Expansionism in American History.* New York: Johns Hopkins University Press, 1958.

THINGS TO NOTICE ABOUT THIS PAPER

This paper is more a historiographic essay than some traditional history papers. Nonetheless, it still presents primary sources, secondary sources, and the interpretations of the author to arrive at a thesis: that "Manifest Destiny" was not just a phenomenon of American history. The paper is more than a mere collection of sources, pasted together. The writer has thought about the material and has arrived at some interpretations that help explain it. She has inferred much from her sources and has treated some of the writings of philosophers and historians as primary sources, as she should.

The author's own point of view is unmistakable: She points out a long-standing interpretation of American history—one which has sometimes captured the popular imagination—and indicates how her interpretation differs. She identifies the source of the phrase and then traces the essential idea back through English history to its ancient roots. She arrives at a judgment about the effect of this on the history of the United States, but she does not preach to the reader. A historian can make judgments on whether certain ideas or actions in the past were good or bad. Historians do that sort of thing all the time. But it is not acceptable in the field of history to rage about events in the past as if your readers must be more persuaded by your emotions than by your evidence and your reasoning. Trust your readers. They do not read this paper to see how upset or self-righteous the writer is; they read to see how a fundamental idea about American history actually ties the United States into a broad reach of global history.

The paper is documented throughout, which means that readers may look up the evidence should they want to know more about it. Notice particularly how Ms. Sonnenburg has used primary sources, some located on the Internet and others identified in the writings of others. This helps prevent the paper from being a collage of what other historians have written about manifest destiny. This technique is highly valuable, especially when you face limitations of direct access to the original primary sources. The thoughtfulness of the author in dealing with her sources is enough to make us feel that we have learned something important from someone who has taken pains to become an authority on an important aspect of U.S. history and to see how it has larger historical implications.

Answer the questions below by studying this sample paper. You would do well to ask these questions about your own writing:

Writer's Checklist

_____ ✔ What sentence or sentences near the beginning of the paper announce the writer's thesis, the main idea that controls the paper?

_____ ✔ How does the writer use quotations? Why does she use shorter quotations, rather than larger block quotations, throughout? Where does see seem to use paraphrase instead?

_____ ✔ What form do footnotes take? Why does the form sometimes change?

_____ ✔ Where does the writer use secondary sources? Can you show where she disagrees with some of her secondary sources?

_____ ✔ Where does the author make inferences? That is, where does she make plausible suggestions about the meaning of various texts when the meaning is not explicit in the text itself?

_____ ✔ Which paragraphs in the essay are primarily narrative? Where does the author write in a more expository mode?

_____ ✔ Where are arguments in the essay?

_____ ✔ Where does the writer make her own judgments clear?

_____ ✔ Where does the author use simile and metaphor to good effect?

_____ ✔ In what ways does the conclusion of the paper mirror some of the ideas in the opening?

APPENDIX B

■ ■ ■

Book Reviews

An essential part of the historian's profession, book reviews represent an assessment of the writing of other historians. Writing book reviews is also a good way to train yourself in understanding how the discipline of history works. Such writing is often complicated and demanding. Reviewers do report on the content of the book, but they also evaluate the work by discussing matters such as the author's logic and organization, evidence and conclusions, and sometimes even the writer's style.

REVIEWING AS A SPECIAL FORM OF WRITING

While writing a book review does require many of the same writing skills we have discussed in this book, it is also a special form of historical writing. You are expected to engage with the historical ideas of another author, to report on and evaluate them, and to present your conclusions to other historians. Such an effort will draw you into debates about historical subjects. That is why many students are asked to write book reviews in their history classes. But keep in mind there are several types of book reviews; for convenience, we refer to them as popular, academic, and scholastic reviews.

Popular reviews are generally written for publications intended for an informed readership, such as the *Atlantic, Harper's, The New Republic,* the *New York Review of Books,* or other widely circulated magazines. Some newspapers, such as the the *New York Times* and the *Washington Post,* also carry similar reviews in some of their editions. Occasionally popular reviews range far and wide, often extending beyond the contents of the book to issues which it raises in the reviewer's mind. Thus some popular reviews take the form of extended essays on particular subjects, which either include the topic of the book or books under review or even occasionally narrower aspects of that topic. While these are frequently very interesting essays, they do not always offer very practical models for the types of reviews you may be asked to write.

Two other types of book reviews are more important as guides to your own writing. The first, which we call *academic* reviews, usually appear in professional journals such as *The American Historical Review,* the *Journal of World History,* or *The Historian.* These are frequently much shorter than popular reviews—often little more than five hundred words—and are generally intended for a scholarly audience. On occasion, historical journals may also publish one or two longer "review essays" that more closely approximate what we have termed popular reviews. But for historians, these review essays frequently focus on the important scholarly issues raised by the book or books the reviewer is considering. We suggest that you look at the book reviews, and review essays, in historical journals and also at the H-Net Reviews Web site, http://www.h-net.org/reviews; these will give you some idea of the way historians generally prepare and present book reviews.

As an example of an academic review, intended for a professional audience of historians, here is a review written for the *Journal of American History* by historian Edward Countryman:

The Shoemaker and the Tea Party: Memory and the American Revolution. By Alfred F. Young. (Boston: Beacon, 1999. xx, 262 pp. $24-00, ISBN 0-8070-7140-4.)

"Gem-like" is one of the highest terms of praise in Alfred F. Young's vocabulary. I have heard him apply it only twice. Almost two decades ago he published a gem-like extended essay called "George Robert Twelves Hewes: A Boston Shoemaker and the Memory of the American Revolution" in the *William and Mary Quarterly*. The essay won that journal's annual best-article prize. Now, as part of an ongoing project about the intertwined themes of revolutionary Boston and historical memory, he has turned that essay into a book.

Part I of *The Shoemaker and the Tea Party* reprints the original essay, broken now into twelve short chapters and slightly amended in the light of Young's thinking since 1982. Part 2 considers how the shoemaker Hewes became a living subject of historical memory in his very old age and how the events in which he took part emerged as an iconic part of revolutionary historical imagery. Taking as his subject what ought to have been obvious (but, as so often happens, was not obvious at all), Young notes the more-than-coincidence of the emergence of the term "tea party" to describe the destruction of the East India Company's tea in December 1773 and the emergence of Hewes as one of the party's/destruction's hallowed veterans six decades later.

It seems unlikely that a revolution-era specialist is unaware of Young's original essay, but a summary remains appropriate. Influenced by the work of E. P. Thompson and Carlo Ginzburg, Young set out to explore the Revolution's meaning in the life of one very ordinary man, who proved under close examination to be extraordinary. Hewes was a "nobody" all his life, until, in very old age, he had his Warholian moment of celebrity. He was born poor in Boston, lived poor there and in New York State, and died poor. There is no little irony in the fact that after the Revolution his loyalist brother Shubael, not he, acquired the honorific "gentleman" to put after his name. But in experiential terms Hewes was rich. He moved from shaking with fear at the very thought of being in John Hancock's house to facing down arrogant officers (British and American alike) and talking on equal terms with George Washington. If life brought Hewes disappointment in material terms, it taught him a great deal about equality.

Young's long-term project has been to recover a revolutionary American Revolution. But, like Thompson, he never has allowed perspective to turn into wishful thinking. He demonstrates that the destruction of the tea was an entirely revolutionary act and that Hewes lived a revolutionary life. He also shows how the late-life fame of Hewes served conservative political purposes. That need not have been so. Other possibilities for historical memory existed, and the life of Hewes could have made good sense within the framework those possibilities provided.

"Definitive" is not in my professional vocabulary. But this elegant book does deserve the description gem-like. The popular success it already enjoys suggests that a public that is hungry for history that is both good and accessible recognizes that point.[1]

You can recognize Professor Countryman's admiration in this review. But you also get a real sense that the reviewer has understood the purpose as well as the historiographic context of the book he is reviewing. Reviews you may be asked to write in one or more of your courses should bear some similarities to this example; we refer to these class assignments as *scholastic* reviews. They are generally longer than most academic reviews but are also intended for a more scholarly audience—your instructors and fellow students. In some ways, they are much more like the "review essays" we mentioned above which sometimes appear in scholarly journals. Your instructor may provide very specific instructions about what should appear in such a review; if so, heed them. But here are some general guidelines that should help you in writing better book reviews no matter what your specific instructions may be.

1. **Read the book!** That may seem self-evident, but it remains perhaps the most important advice about writing a book review. Now and then even professional historians don't read the books they review in journals. You can see their errors when outraged authors write to protest; occasionally you will find such communications in historical journals. Don't let that happen to you! If you find and read one or more academic reviews of the book you have been assigned

---

[1] Edward Countryman, review of *The Shoemaker and the Tea Party,* by Alfred F. Young, *Journal of American History,* 87(2000): 648–649.

or have selected to review, you may learn a great deal. But that is not a substitute for reading the book and making your own judgments. Also remember this: Fundamental honesty requires for you to say if you take something—ideas or quotations—for your book review from a review someone else has written. Our cautions about plagiarism apply to book reviews as well!

2. **Identify the author, but don't waste time on needless or extravagant claims about her or him.** It is a cliché to say that the author is "well qualified" to write a book; such a comment adds little to your review. You may write briefly about the author's background and experience, perhaps the work he or she put into creating the book you are reviewing. But don't belabor the point.

3. **Always give the author's major theme or thesis, his or her motive for writing the book.** What is your assessment of that theme or thesis? Read the book thoughtfully. Always read the introduction or the preface. Students in a hurry may skip the introduction, thinking they are saving time. That can be a serious mistake. Authors often use introductions to state the reasons that impelled them to write their books. Indeed, we recommend you read the preface, the introduction, and the last chapter of a book before you read the complete work. Few writers can bear to leave their books without a parting shot: they want to be sure readers get the point! Reviewers should take advantage of that impulse.

Some of our students object to our advice that they read the last chapter first. We remind them that history books are not novels, and good history books—as well as shorter essays—almost never have surprise endings. By reading the last chapter, you see where the author is heading as you read the entire book. And always remember the terms "theme" and "thesis" are not quite the same as the subject. The subject of the book may be the biography of

Winston Churchill, prime minister of Great Britain during World War II. The theme or thesis, however, may be that Churchill was a great wartime leader but a poor interpreter of the postwar world.

4. **Summarize, but only briefly, the evidence the author presents in support of the thesis.** Do not fall into the habit of writing a summary of the book as if you were writing a report rather than a review. This approach seldom can be translated into a successful book *review*. Don't try to report every interesting detail in the book. Leave something for readers to discover on their own. But it frequently is a good idea to recount some interesting incidents. Tell a story or two from the book. You may also wish to consider the types of evidence the author has used and particularly the effort to rely upon primary sources.

5. **Consider quoting a line or two here and there in your review to give the flavor of the text.** Quote selectively but fairly. The prose of the author you review may help spice up your own review. But avoid long chunks of quotation. You must show your readers that you have absorbed the book you review.

6. **Avoid lengthy comments about the style of the book.** It is fine to say that the style is good, bad, interesting, or tedious. If a book is especially well written or if it is incomprehensible, you may quote a sentence to illustrate a good or bad style, but don't belabor the point. Generalizations such as, "This book is interesting," or "This book is boring," do little to enhance your review. If you do your job in the review, readers can tell whether you find it interesting or boring. And remember, if you are bored, the fault might be in you rather than the book. An Ancient History professor at the University of Tennessee, when one of us said reading the Greek philosopher Plutarch was boring, declared sternly, "Mr. Marius, you have no right to be bored with Plutarch." Both of us agree he was right.

7. **Don't feel compelled to say negative things about the book.** If you find inaccuracies, say so. If you disagree with the writer's interpretation here and there, say that too, giving your reasons. However, you should avoid passionate attacks on the book. Scholarship is not always courteous, but it should be. Reviewers who launch savage attacks on books usually make fools of themselves. Remember, too, that petty complaints about the book may also make you look foolish or unfair. Do not waste time pointing out typos unless they change the meaning the author intends. Always remember that every good book has flaws. The author may make some minor errors in fact or some questionable judgments. Even so, the book may be extremely valuable. Don't condemn a book outright because you find some mistakes. Try to judge the book as a whole.

8. **Review the book the author has written.** You may wish the author had written a different book. You might write a different book yourself. But the author has written *this* book. If the book did not need to be written, if it adds nothing to our knowledge of the field, if it makes conclusions unwarranted by the evidence, say so. But don't review the book as if it should be another book.

9. **Try to bring something from your own experience— your reading, your thoughts, your reflections, your recollections—to your review.** If you are reviewing a book about early twentieth-century China, and if you have been fortunate enough to have traveled in China, you may bring your own impressions to the review of the book. Try to make use of a broad part of your education when you review a book. If you have read other books in other classes that are relevant to this class, say something about those books in your review. If you know facts the author has overlooked, say so. But avoid writing as if you possess independent knowledge of the author's subject when in fact you have taken all you know from the book itself. Don't pretend to be an expert when you are not. Be honest.

A SAMPLE STUDENT REVIEW

The following review, also of Alfred Young's *The Shoemaker and the Tea Party*, was written by a student. Consider how this review differs from that of Professor Countryman and also how it touches on many of the same points.

A Common Man and the American Revolution

A Review of Alfred F. Young, *The Shoemaker and the Tea Party: Memory and the American Revolution*

BY SABRINA SHILAD
East Tennessee State University
February 26, 2005
History 4037: The American Revolution
Professor Dale Schmitt

Alfred F. Young's 1999 book, *The Shoemaker and the Tea Party,* allows him to express his views on the American Revolution and the position that a common man would take during this time. The book is divided into two sections; the first part traces the life of George Robert Twelves Hewes, and the second half deals with the impact of the revolution concerning the town of Boston and how this relates to George Robert Twelves Hewes. The book gives a clear insight about what it would have been like to be a common mechanic in Boston during revolutionary times.

Alfred F. Young spent close to twenty years working on *The Shoemaker and the Tea Party*. Young became interested in the American Revolution when he was a graduate student at Columbia University. He obtained his doctorate at Northwestern University, where specialized in American history. Young then taught in several different universities in Connecticut, New Jersey, and Illinois. Since 1990, he has been a senior research fellow at the

Newberry Library. The predecessor to Young's book was an essay published in the *William and Mary Quarterly* in 1981. The success of the essay in the academic community spurred Young to give a second life to the essay and to make *The Shoemaker and the Tea Party* accessible to a broader audience.

The book begins by introducing the reader to George Robert Twelves Hewes. He is first presented through the two major biographies written about him in 1834 and 1835. Both of these two books describe him to be the last surviving participant in the Boston Tea Party. These two biographies are significant because they are the first recorded instances in which the destruction of the tea was called the Boston Tea Party. James Hawkes and Benjamin Bussey Thatcher, the original two biographers, "sifted" through the memories of the old man, ninety-three at the time, to retrieve the reminiscences and feelings from sixty to eighty years earlier.

George Robert Twelves Hewes was born in 1742 to a poor tanner in Boston. He was the sixth of nine children, but only three older brothers and one younger brother survived childhood. Hewes was a very active boy and frequently got into trouble. The violent punishments he received as a child formed in him a very kind mind that did not want to see anyone harmed. Because there was no one to help pay for his apprenticeship in a respectable profession, Hewes was apprenticed to a shoemaker, which was considered one of the lower mechanic jobs that one could acquire.

Hewes was involved in three of the most significant acts in late colonial and revolutionary Boston: the massacre, tea party, and tarring and feathering John Malcolm. In the massacre, Hewes was an unarmed protester who caught James Caldwell after James was injured. Hewes chose to observe the events of the massacre without becoming a participant. However, Hewes was actively involved in the tea party and was one of the "semi-invited" men who destroyed the British East India Company's tea. He was given a slightly elevated rank on the ships by the Sons of Liberty due to his ability to whistle loudly. While on the ship, Hewes believed that he helped to throw a chest of tea overboard with John Hancock. Further, one might go so far as to say that Hewes was partly responsible for the tarring and feathering of John Malcolm. Malcolm threatened to beat a small boy with a cane for running into him. Hewes stopped Malcolm and Hewes was then clobbered over the head by Malcolm. The mob then proceeded to strip Malcolm and tar and feather him. Ironically, when Hewes awoke from his forced slumber, he ran after the mob attempting to cover Malcolm's naked body with a blanket.

Hewes became well known for his long name and short stature. Only 5'1", he was too short to enlist in the military. However, Hewes later became involved in the militia, serving for a total of twenty months in a variety of capacities. During the time of his militia service he was married to Sally Sumner, a wash-woman, who produced for him sixteen children. As a militia seaman, Hewes was supposed to have opportunities to make money— through buccaneer activities—to help support his wife and family. However, he made very little money on these voyages because the captains cheated him and would not pay him or give him his share of the bounty. Hewes was a poor man for most of his life and had to be supported by his children in his elder years.

The second portion of the book focused on the entire town of Boston and how the public viewed each of the major events. Young emphasizes public remembrance of the revolution and the how the memory was shaped in the public mind. The controlling bodies of the city forced much of Boston to forget the events of the revolution by only emphasizing particular events and forcing many holidays to go uncelebrated. Individual people and actions were erased from memories and all that was remembered was that George Washington saved the nation.

Alfred Young's biography of George Robert Twelves Hewes is very well written and allows the reader to easily follow along. The writing style that Young uses made the book seemingly enjoyable to read and allowed the reader to stay focused on the book. The reader actually became involved in Hewes's story, wondering what Hewes was going to do next. Young avoided verbose sentences and presented his points in a very simple manner.

Most readers know about the examples Young uses in the book. This prevented the reader from becoming overwhelmed with dates, events, and people. Commonly, historical writers assume that the reader has a well-developed knowledge on the subject, leaving the average reader lost in an abyss of names. Young avoids this dilemma by simplifying his explanations of the revolutionary acts mentioned in his book.

Young, however, throughout the beginning of the book draws extensively from the other two biographies written about Hewes. The quotations from Thatcher's and Hawkes's biographies on Hewes seemed excessively long and frequent. It becomes so excessive that the reader may consider reading the other biographies as opposed to spending time with Young's summation of the other books.

The most powerful aspect of the book is its explanation of how the lower class citizen in Boston reacted to the "legendary" events surrounding the Revolution. This is significant because there is very little documentation about the concerns of simple people during the Revolution. The problems with money, illness, and having a successful business are all addressed in Young's book. The reader becomes aware how challenging it was to support a family on a meager income. Young also explains to the reader alternative ways of making money that were necessary to survive, such as fishing for the soldiers and working for the militia.

Alfred F. Young's book was very educational and helpful. The book could explain details of the revolution to the average person without causing mystification or confusion. *The Shoemaker and the Tea Party* was an outstanding biography and analysis of the events in Boston before the official beginning of the revolution as well as how the city reacted after the revolution. Young's book clearly shows what revolutionary life was like for the common, poor man—the mechanics, as they were called—and to what extent the common people would have been involved in riotous demonstrations.

THINGS TO NOTICE ABOUT THESE REVIEWS

In comparing the two reviews presented here, first consider what they have in common. Notice how both focus on some details about the personal life of the subject of this biography and how they recognize the efforts of the book's author to place his subject in a larger historical context. Which of the reviews deals most with the details of the person who is the subject of the book? And which is more concerned about the historiographic place of the book itself in the study of American history? Can you recognize some of the differences between an academic review and a scholastic review from studying these two examples?

As you make these comparisons, think about the key questions below. You might also use them to advantage in examining the book reviews that you write.

Writer's Checklist

_____ ✔ Have these reviewers given evidence they have read the book?

_____ ✔ Is the main theme or thesis of the book adequately identified?

_____ ✔ Are both the evidence and the argument used to support the central thesis of the book clear?

_____ ✔ Is the writing style of the book's author appropriately considered?

_____ ✔ Would quotations from the book help in giving the readers of the reviews a better sense of the writing style?

_____ ✔ Are the judgments of the book both temperate and sound?

_____ ✔ Is the book being reviewed the book that was written?

_____ ✔ Has either reviewer succeeded in bringing something personal to the review?

APPENDIX C

■ ■ ■

Short Writing Assignments

In many history courses you may be asked to write short essays, often on very specific topics. For example, we frequently ask our students to write short essays—usually no more than about 500 words (or two printed pages)—about a portion of reading we have assigned for a course. These essays, and many similar assignments, are intended to encourage thoughtful reading of some document, historical essay, or even a journal article and to stimulate careful consideration of it in a written essay. Often these assignments are made well in advance so you may plan your reading and studying accordingly. Sometimes they may be announced just prior to your reading or studying the material about which you are expected to write. On other occasions, very similar questions may be the basis for essay examinations, requiring you to reflect seriously on what you have been studying.

One such advanced notice assignments we have used is based on students reading an excerpt from the royal chronicle of the Christian monarch, Amda Seyon, who ruled Ethiopia from 1314 to 1344. We ask students to write a 500 word essay comparing Amda Seyon's efforts in resisting Islamic invasions to similar situations in

Europe and elsewhere at about the same time. In another assignment, sometimes introduced in class as an immediate prelude to discussion, we invite students to study the famous Jan van Eyck painting of 1434, *Giovanni Arnolfini and His Bride*. Then we ask them to write a short essay about the objects van Eyck depicts and how they offer evidence concerning the social standing of merchants in medieval Europe.[1]

These brief essays are somewhat different from other kinds of (usually longer) essays we have discussed in this book; they are actually more like essay examinations, to be written within a given time in circumstances where you must rely on your memory, usually without the aid of notes, books, or the reference room of a library. Essay exams test what you know and how you think about what you know. They are to some degree artificial creations; historians usually do not write under the strictures of the standard essay exam format. They write and revise, go back to their sources, and revise some more. So essay exams frequently are the most comprehensive test of how much you have learned in a history course. They are so much a part of the Western academic scene that you doubtless already have much experience with them. The best examinations allow you to show your knowledge about the facts, demonstrate some recall of sources for these facts, and prove that you can make judgments about them.

Perhaps the best way to prepare to write any of these short essays, including exams, is to study the readings you have been assigned, attend class diligently, and take good notes. The best way to take notes—from classes or readings—is to jot down important concepts, using keywords and phrases but not trying to take down every word. As soon as you can after class or a period of reading, sit down at your computer or your notepad and, using these original notes as your foundation, write out an account of what the professor

------

[1] Copies of both these documents and introductory discussions of each can be found in Dennis Sherman et al., *World Civilizations: Sources, Images, and Interpretations*, 3d ed. (New York: McGraw-Hill, 2002), 230–231, 243–244.

said or what you read. When something is unclear, ask what the point was; use reference books, and especially your textbooks, to make sure you understand the information. All this takes time, of course, and college students are busy, many of them working at jobs to support themselves in school. It is hard to take the time to go over notes shortly after taking them. Yet if you force yourself to do so, you will discover that you may save time in the long run. You will impress the information on your brain as you write out your notes about it. You will become acquainted with your own notes, and when time for writing a short essay assignment or taking an essay exam draws near, you can face it without cramming just ahead of time because you will already know most of the material. You might get together with classmates and come up with a collection of class notes—from lectures and your reading—that you have all cooperated in putting together. In our experience, students who study together and talk about the class are more likely to make the highest grades on their essays. In our opinion, this is not deceitful but rather a reflection of the cooperative spirit of much historical work.

If you receive the question for a short essay ahead of time, study it. If you only receive the question shortly before you begin to write, you can still be prepared for what questions you do receive. Pay particular attention to what your professor emphasizes in class. Try to think what questions you would ask if you were that professor. Remember, professors usually feel that if they have spent a good long time discussing a subject in class, it is only fair to expect students to know something about it! If you write out questions of your own, you will be surprised at how well you sometimes can read your professor's mind. Once you have the question for your essay, follow the directions carefully. *Read the questions.* We have always been surprised at how often students will read questions carelessly and write an essay having almost nothing to do with the topic.

In looking at the questions, determine what mode of historical writing each of them calls for. Your primary task may be to tell a story: "Trace the career of Martin Luther from the Indulgence Controversy of 1517 to his appearance before the Diet of Worms in

1521." You will need to narrate a sequence of events from 1517 to 1521, being careful to choose the most important steps in this part of Luther's career. Or you may be asked to explain the historical significance of an event, a document, or a person: "Discuss the significance of the heroic image of Sunyatsen in the developing ideologies of Chinese Communism and its 'Nationalist' opponents." To answer this question you must prepare an exposition that will first explain the "heroic image" of Sunyatsen as he became the leader in the effort to free the Chinese from European imperialist control. Then you will need to tell what his program for China included and how it changed as first the Communists under Mao Zedong and then the rival Kuomintang Party under Chiang Kai-shek took over his message for their own ends. You can complete your exposition by indicating why and how these changes were significant in China's history.

Related to questions about significance are comparison questions which many history professors are fond of asking. In effect, the professor gets two answers from you for the price of one question! And you are required to demonstrate the flexibility of your mind and the quantity of your knowledge about two portions of the course material. For example: "Compare Thomas More's *Utopia* and Machiavelli's *The Prince,* both written in 1516." Again, you will need to write an exposition, in this case one that explains the key ideas in both books, recognizing that both More and Machiavelli were preoccupied with reform. You will also want to emphasize that there were differences in the kind of reform each wanted. And you can conclude by evaluating how each reform program affected the world of medieval Europe. In making this comparison you can, in addition, explain how radically different two people, living at the same time in similar cultures, can be so different.

Other short essay questions may ask that you argue a point. These essays are difficult and challenging. You might given a question much like this: "Which African national leader of the 1960s provided the best program of government for his nation in the two decades following its independence from colonial control? What arguments would you make to support your choice?" Whether you select Kwame Nkrumah, Julius Nyerere, or another African leader, you would need to construct your essay making a plausible case for whomever you decide to write about. But remember, historians seldom prove anything beyond any doubt. You cannot resolve every uncertainty and eliminate all contrary opinions in the limited space you have for a short essay, and certainly not in the few minutes you have to write an examination. You can, however, show that you know the material, have thought about it intelligently, and can offer a cogent rationale for what it means. As always in an argument, you should show some familiarity with viewpoints contrary to your own and provide a few words about why you reject them.

Among our favorite short essay questions are those asking students to analyze an important text. Your professor may give you a paragraph from a noteworthy historical document and ask you to write about what it means. Such questions could also be more focused than that. One question that we recently posed for students was this:

> The European philosopher, Francis Bacon, observed in the early seventeenth century that "the force and virtue and consequences of discoveries . . . are to be seen nowhere more conspicuously than these three which were unknown to the ancients. . . namely, printing, gunpowder, and the compass. For these have changed the whole face and state of things throughout the world." Would you agree with Bacon that the development and spread of these technological innovations had such a profound impact on world history?

This question not only requires a student to think carefully about some very specific things, but also demands consideration of their significance. One of our students, Bill Hembrock, wrote a short essay answering this question in a recent examination for a course on "World History to 1500":

> All three of these discoveries were brought to the West from China where they had been invented

during the Tang and Song dynasties. Once known there, they played a significant role in advancing Europe's power around the globe after 1500, just as Bacon suggested.

The gunpowder chemistry originally developed in China was not a very effective military weapon. It was brought to the West with the Mongol conquerors, as Bentley and Ziegler describe in *Traditions and Encounters* [the course textbook], where the technology was refined and the first crude cannons were used in battle. Later sailors and explorers from Europe were able to advance the technology to assist in conquering people in their explorations and empire building, such as the Portuguese in Africa, the Spanish in Central, South, and North America, and the British in India.

The magnetic compass was also invented in China but, as the text also points out, was spread first throughout the Indian Ocean by Indian and African sailors who used the compass and the trade winds to facilitate a great deal of trade throughout the Indian Ocean, from northern Africa, eastern Africa, and India on to southeast Asia and China. Eventually the knowledge got to the European navigators, who used it to explore the rest of the oceans of the world and finally tie the whole world together. From then on trade and exchange of ideas, diseases, customs, and religions could be exchanged from anywhere in the world to any other part of the globe.

Printing, the text again notes, was invented in China, but taken from its Asian roots and advanced by Europeans. Printing helped agriculture improve in Europe in the thirteenth through fifteenth centuries by spreading information about new techniques on raising different crops. The printing of the Bible also helped spread the faith and unify the Christian world. Europe was united by Christianity, with the church exerting great authority over the people through scriptural authority, common beliefs, and church practices.

Europe had been a fractured area politically,
and backward compared to other great empires of
the world especially after the collapse of the
Roman Empire. By taking these three inventions and
adapting them for their needs and advancement,
European countries became the discoverers and
creators of great empires of the post-1500 world.

Notice how the author begins with a short paragraph offering a thesis statement that refers specifically to the text quoted within the question. He follows this with separate paragraphs on each of the three discoveries Bacon mentions, analyzing the significance of each. And he concludes his argument by referring again to his thesis. He also mentions the textbook assigned for the course, where he found much of his information; this is much the same as the citations to sources you would provide in a longer essay.

Achieving this balance in any short essay requires study and preparation in advance, and then careful planning when you first receive the question. We encourage students to jot down quickly words and phrases they remember concerning the question, and then to reorganize that collage of ideas into a basic outline. For an examination especially, you must do this quickly and also carefully judge how much time you can spend on each part of an examination. Take care not to spend too much of your time organizing—or on writing one part of an essay or answering only one of several questions asked on an exam. After completing your college education you will discover that allocating time is one of the most essential tasks of a human being; efficient use of time in writing examination essays is good training for what will come later on.

Managing your time and the space available is, of course, an important part of writing any history essay. Yet even in a very short essay, whether during an exam or not, you need to be as specific as possible. You must name people, dates, documents, places—answering the basic historian's questions: Who? What? When? Where? Why? These questions should haunt your mind, and you should always be trying to answer them as you read and write. Plan your work carefully to be certain you can complete those tasks. Doing so will help you prepare to answer any history question. You likely will discover that time spent considering them—even before you know what questions you may need to write about—offers you an opportunity to shape your knowledge, integrate various parts of it, and produce an essay (even on an examination!) that may be not only a source of pleasure but also of pride.

As you complete any short history essay, including those you may write for an essay examination, read over what you have written before you submit it. Take enough time to consider the key questions below.

Writer's Checklist

_____ ✔ Have I sharply focused my topic?

_____ ✔ Have I made a clearly stated argument?

_____ ✔ Have I carefully acknowledged the sources of ideas and evidence?

_____ ✔ Have I included my own original thoughts?

_____ ✔ Have I expressed myself clearly?

SELECT BIBLIOGRAPHY OF STUDENT RESOURCES

∎ ∎ ∎

Appleby, Joyce, Lynn Hunt, and Margaret Jacob. *Telling the Truth About History*. New York: W. W. Norton, 1994.

A challenging and sometimes provocative consideration of history as practiced by American historians at the end of the twentieth century.

Arnold, John. *History: A Very Short Introduction*. Oxford and New York: Oxford University Press, 2000.

Short yet thoughtful considerations of a few basic issues confronting historians as they write about the past.

Barzun, Jacques. *On Writing, Editing, and Publishing: Essays Explicative and Horatory*, 2d ed. Chicago: University of Chicago Press, 1986.

A collection of essays written between 1950 and 1985 by American historian Jacques Barzun, including consideration of "A Writer's Discipline" (pp. 5–17).

———. *Simple and Direct: A Rhetoric for Writers*, 4th ed. New York: Quill, 2001.

A somewhat philosophical approach to writing, with excellent suggestions from an accomplished historian and writer.

Berger, Stefan, Heiko Feldner, and Kevin Passmore, eds. *Writing History: Theory and Practice*. London: Arnold, 2003.

Sixteen essays examining problems, issues, and examples some historians have encountered when writing about history.

Brundage, Anthony. *Going to the Sources: A Guide to Historical Research and Writing*, 3d ed. Wheeling, IL: Harlan Davidson, 2002.

Nearly twenty percent of this very brief guide is taken up with an excellent treatment of writing a historiographic essay, including a student essay.

Feinstein, Charles H., and Mark Thomas. *Making History Count: A Primer in Quantitative Methods for Historians*. New York: Cambridge University Press, 2002.

Considered by some historians to be the best introduction to the subject for their discipline and therefore highly recommended for students.

Gaddis, John Lewis. *The Landscape of History: How Historians Map the Past.* New York: Oxford University Press, 2002.

> Contends that the modern practice of history is more akin to new scientific fields, such as geology and evolutionary biology, than the social and political sciences.

Grafton, Anthony. *The Footnote: A Curious History,* rev. ed. Cambridge, MA: Harvard University Press, 1977.

> An engaging history of scholarly attribution by a distinguished American historian.

Hughes-Warrington, Marnie. *Fifty Key Thinkers on History.* London and New York: Routledge, 2000.

> Brief intellectual biographies offering a guide to the practice of history from ancient times until the present, although forty percent of the historians considered were born in the twentieth century.

Lukacs, John. *A Student's Guide to the Study of History.* Wilmington, DE: ISI Books, 2000.

> Written by a distinguished, culturally conservative historian, this is only a brief overview of the discipline and its attractions.

Marwick, Arthur. *The New Nature of History: Knowledge, Evidence, Language.* Chicago: Lyceum Books, 2001.

> Thirty years after preparing a guide to *The Nature of History,* a British historian reflects on the changes in the practice and writing of history.

Munslow, Alan. *The Routledge Companion to Historical Studies.* London and New York, 2000.

> A twenty-first century perspective, with nearly sixty entries on many key topics of interest to beginning historians; includes an extensive bibliography keyed to the entries.

Southgate, Beverley. *What Is History For?* New York and London: Routledge, 2005.

> A senior British historian examines the uses of history, with examples from the past as well as suggestions for future directions in historical writing.

Staley, David J. *Computers, Visualization, and History: How New Technology Will Transform Our Understanding of the Past.* Armonk, NY: M. E. Sharpe, 2003.

> Based on a sympathetic understanding of the potential that new technologies have to influence the presentation of historical knowledge, this book will challenge readers with new insights on the treatment of the past.

Tuchman, Barbara W. *Practicing History: Selected Essays.* New York: Ballantine Books, 1982.

> Selections from nearly fifty years of writing by a prize-winning historian on the craft, its discipline, and its implications for society.

CREDITS

■ ■ ■

INDEX

■ ■ ■